Love
From
Nell
December
2012 .

The Sheffield Anthology
Poems from the City Imagined

The Sheffield Anthology
Poems from the City Imagined

Edited by
**Agnes Lehoczky, Adam Piette,
Ann Sansom, Peter Sansom**

smith|doorstop

Published 2012 by
Smith/Doorstop Books
The Poetry Business
Bank Street Arts
32-40 Bank Street
Sheffield S1 2DS
www.poetrybusiness.co.uk

ISBN 978-1-906613-61-7

British Library Cataloguing-in-Publication Data.
A catalogue record for this book is available from the British Library.

Typeset by Utter
Printed by Lightning Source
Cover design by Utter
Cover photo: The 'Cutting Edge' sculpture at Sheaf Square,
Sheffield Midland Station.

We would like to thank the following publishers for permission to reprint some of the poems here:
Anvil Press Poetry, Bloodaxe Books, Carcanet Press, Enitharmon Press, Faber & Faber, Flambard
Press, Picador Poetry (Pan Macmillan) and Smith|Doorstop Books. Also the magazines, journals
and anthologies where some of the poems were first published. For permission to reprint the poem
by William Empson, we are grateful to the Empson estate and to Curtis Brown Ltd. We apologise
for any omissions or/and inadvertant infringement of copyright, which we will correct in any future
edition from the comfort of our cell.

Smith/Doorstop Books is a member of Inpress,
www.inpressbooks.co.uk. Distributed by Central Books Ltd.,
99 Wallis Road, London E9 5LN.

Generously funded by the University of Sheffield's Festival of the Mind
The Poetry Business is an Arts Council National Portfolio Organisation

Contents

Preface

There is a cycle in the life of cities, boom and bust, regeneration to depression, mad urban planning to sad dereliction – and in most big cities these cycles have different lag effects in different zones, some patches of town remaining moribund whilst others gain prestige and pot luck. The capitalist, industrial cities of the north have seen the most extraordinary rollercoaster arcs, from the fantastic fiery furnace of production in the 19th century through wartime booms, then down, down, down, crumbling and exhausted, to post-industrial wasteland, followed by fitful acts of postmodern reinvention with associated service industry contortions, government scheming, flashy corporate, hypermarket, supermall, cultural regeneration. Something of the social energy that goes into these mysterious collective processes attaches itself to the language and mores of the northern cities, either as remnant, resistance, nostalgia, or underground, city-street bravado.

Sheffield has been blasted and battered and retooled enough to baffle the bland sociological gaze. It commands respect in both its clapped-out doggedness and in the jumped-up energy of the bustling, partying youthfulness of its Saturday nights: the contradiction not one at all once the streets are allowed their say, rather than the patronizing interiors of the banks and culture halls. The energy of the voices from Fargate to Crookes, Gleadless to Attercliffe, Walkley to Heeley, Tinsley to Nether Edge, the abiding buzz of historical memory – steel industry, blitz, miners' strike – the lugubrious brio of the stories of development and struggle at each villagey borough, the criss-crossing of family, political, ethnic and class forces, the music, the pubs and dives and football clubs, the draw of the parks and hills and Peak, the tramstop debates, the student whizzbang craziness down Division Street, the sudden differences as one walks up and down those steep backstreets from clattery to leafy to luxurious to pokey Victorian suburbia: Sheffield has many lives of its own, and gives them with an anarchic friendly largesse that couldn't give a chuff what you do with it all.

The anthology hopes it gives some sense of that anarchic energy in the host of voices gathered, the kinds of stories told, the strange visions and glimpses behind scenes visualized in these many lines. A poem can seem to be little more than an anecdote well told, or a little tale buffed up by fancy talk. But if they are poems, they are also parcels of imagination-in-language, and as such give us an amalgam of the city. They fuse together the city as imagined by a specific consciousness at a specific time, with the expansive, often comic, always transformative story-told city of Sheffield citizens as a collective. Those two cities, the poet's corner of town and the citizen city as a social energy field, come together and fuse to create a hybrid which will carry intimations of a third city: the city of the imagination, city as hive of words, speaking as many, as ensemble, orchestration of strange, dissonant, and variously tuneful harmonies of this our metropolis. This anthology hopes to help the urban music-making happen: and offers the Sheffield meditations and games of the mind written by these 101 poets to the city as a gift of language (with more rattle than a can of mabs) that we hope will both inspire and abide as a book both companionable and urbane for the many Sheffields of the future.

– Adam Piette

Some Notes on the Selection

Sheffield is blessed, if that's the right word, with a lot of poets; more just now it seems than ever. Many of whom we thought must have written well about the city (we guessed there might be as many as twenty). And so it might be possible to put together an anthology which would map and snapshot a place and its various times in the way that only poems can. Almost at once we found forty poets to include, and we realised there must be others out there as well – and so canvassed friends for writers to approach. In this way the book grew. And grew. At sixty poets, we realised we wanted to be inclusive – and decided to allow poems that were only indirectly about life in Sheffield and environs (though we drew the line at Daljit Nagra's kindly-meant but frankly *West* Yorkshire poem about *Huddersfield*). Even now, with over a hundred poets, we know there will be people we've missed.

We decided early on to include only contemporary writers. 'Contemporary' is a handy term because no-one knows what it means, and so it allows us to reprint poets who are no longer with us, but whose poems certainly are, such as Stanley Cook and George MacBeth. It is stretching a point to include William Empson, but who could resist his 'Masque for the Queen's visit to the city and its University'? We did type up Edward Carpenter's tour-de-force 'Sheffield', but though Carpenter (1846-1929) is an important Sheffield figure kept alive by his 'Friends Of' group, it seemed best to direct readers to Peter Machin's fine anthology, *Sheffield in Verse* (ALD, 2004), 'an illustrated collection of poems, odes, doggerel, ditties and songs', which represents Carpenter and many of the city's older writers, not least Ebeneezer Elliott (1781-1849), 'the corn-law rhymer', and James Montgomery (1771-1854), famous enough for a statue outside the Cathedral and best-remembered for his hymns (including 'Angels from the Realms of Glory'). There is another anthology in the local history library, *Sheffield in Poetry*, edited by Yann Lovelock (Sheffield Festival Publications, 1970). Though much slimmer than the Machin and not as lively, it is just as alive. It is an inspiring read, and is incidentally where we found

Lovelock's own rather brilliant poem about being a toddler in the Sheffield blitz. In his introduction, Lovelock makes the point that 'Sheffield benefits from being a hospitable city capable of taking in outside elements and making them part of itself ... It is this feeling of community that makes Sheffielders out of strangers; and it is this which makes its poetry distinctive.' We know that this is true and that it is what accounts for how varied the present anthology is.

From the start, we wanted to include 'Sheffield' poets who are living elsewhere now or are only here for a while (as students for instance). We knew of several non- or no longer Sheffield poets, whose poems had to be in the book, Sean O'Brien for instance and his fellow Professor of Poetry at Hallam (though originally from Montserrat), the late and much-missed E A Markham. Also we wanted to feature some of the poems that are literally a part of the city, the brilliant Off the Shelf commissions – Andrew Motion's towering 'What If ...', and Roger McGough's poem in the Winter Gardens that ends 'Sheffield, twinned with Mars' (how poetically true that statement is). Just as true to life is Carol Ann Duffy's tender poem that takes her daughter along the Five Weirs Walk. And as true to Sheffield also is Jarvis Cocker's poem with its last line that everyone seems to know, 'Don't they teach you no brains at that school?'.

It has been a pleasure putting together this book, and a real eye-opener. As directors of the Poetry Business, we knew we were fortunate to live in a city of so many fine writers. We just didn't know quite how many fine writers. Thank you to all of them here for allowing us to use their poems.

– Ann and Peter Sansom

Anthony Adler

A View from the Information Commons

Sitting in an armchair in the library by a window
reading *Howl and other poems*, watching my reflection

reading *Howl* (and other poems), watching my reflection
watch the choreography of cars orbit the roundabout

on their way home – waiting patient implacable in ranks
with glowing beaming and unblinking eyes like the angelic host:

wide-loaded lorries lumbering like over-laden manifestos,
the unroadworthy the wheeling wounded

playing pirates, eyepatched, reinventing cyclops.
Nobody did this. "Over there a man is throwing a hat

like a hoopla-ring," and I turn: *Greeks*, he says, *greeks*,
retrieves it, mumbles something I can't hear

because he's isn't talking to me. She leafs through her book, swearing at it,
he wheels his chair somewhere else and notices I'm staring:

I look somewhere else and can't see his reflection,
go back to the carousel through the glass, darkly.

She looks like a hologram, a ghost, an angel
with too many hands, types with too many fingers,

and the host loops round the roundabout sedately,
obdurately, taxi, ambulance, somnambulant.

David Annwn

Radial Version

swansdown the nape
on shale's moor
between medico-legal
& cactus property

fly between corporate
and commons
pluck barbs
from delectable

downpour
through Brook and
thorpe of Nether

Toyota pentagon
bank of flashes

pearling brim
tenting
in leavygreave

gapping swallow
at portobello

stippled exultant
inner outlets
edges feathering
wheatsheaf-field

Charlotte Ansell

Ode to Sheffield

If you're doing nowt, meet me at the fountain,
we'll skulk in the tropics of the Winter Gardens,

listen to the fans go hoarse at Bramall Lane,
ride the tram to Halfway and back again.

Chapeltown, Hillsborough, Gleadless, Malin Bridge,
Grenoside, Greystones, Shalesmoor, Attercliffe.

We'll watch sunlight slant off slate grey stone,
see ancient woodland blanket round terraced homes.

We'll watch a Magic Lantern film, eat pies in Sharrow,
tea at the Rude Shipyard, go to Padley Gorge and paddle.

The Rivelin Valley, Millhouses Park, Eccesall Woods,
Forge Dam, Nether Edge, Heeley City Farm, Crookes.

We'll scour Division Street for tat and vintage dresses,
hang out in Cole Brothers, loiter in Lowedges,

take the kids to swim in rings at Pond's Forge,
window shop on Abbeydale for furniture we can't afford.

Burngreave, Stannington, Atlas, Brightside,
Carter Knowle, Manor Top, Pitsmoor, Ecclesfield.

We'll see pinpoints of light glance off the canal, a towering wheel,
Rough-hewn edges, a centre of glass, mirrors, steel.

And when we're all worn out and the day is at an end,
We'll salute you Sheffield, in all your shabby glory, as a friend.

Simon Armitage

The Holy Land

Christ was born under Tinsley Viaduct –
why not? –
the Leopold being overbooked.

They dipped him in the silver waters
of the Don
until his little hands were forks.

Magi brought gifts from as far away
as Carnaby
and Goole: hair-straighteners,

a replica Louis Vuitton man-bag, a two-piece
snooker cue.
Herod's henchmen sought him out,

hoodies from Bethlehem, PA, but hidden
in a battered
velvet-lined guitar-case, our Saviour slept.

At secondary school he underachieved
but showed
promise in team sports, especially lacrosse.

Pointing to the seven hills he proclaimed:
"There shall I
picnic, there shall I BMX, preach,

sip Special Brew at dusk, find a cure
for cancer
of the lung, walk the dog, and there

on a goalpost shall they nail-gun my palms
and feet.
He asked us, "Who is your Lord? Who's

the boss man around here? Into whose arms
shall you turn?"
We answered, "Thee. Thou. Thine."

Ann Atkinson

The New Allotment

It's here on the plan, she says: a grid
laid out pre-war, hers numbered 223.
Down from the taps, between high hedges,
past pyramids of beans, tomato vines,
maize, compost humming in a daze of wasps,
she counts the doors: parlour doors, shed doors,
front doors, one with a cat-flap, Shangri La,
Beware of the Dog, Eden, then the dog tied up
and docile. She sings along to a somewhere radio,
dum-de-dum-the-archers. It's 222, then 224,
and in between a hawthorn's overgrown her door.

Undeterred, jacket pulled up round her head,
she shoulders through and disappears,
reports back, *brambles, bindweed, dock leaves,
nettles*, her voice more distant, there's a shed,
she's shouting now, roof good, chimney,
donkey-stove. I can hardly hear her.
I'm sitting in the sun eating blackberries.
The radio's a wireless, *music-while-you-work*,
it's dig-for-victory times. I'm spitting seeds
and waiting by the fireweed.
She could be years in there.

Then we drove on

but we had slowed at the same time,
stopped for the stoat on the road between us,
the still calf-lick of its alert, the poised streak
sleek away-through-the-hedge-and-gone of it.

And as we engaged gears we smiled
and waved. So we passed each other
but had shared the moment, witnessed it
clear as morning light and close.
I smiled for miles. I loved his face.

The Best Thing

The best thing in the world
is to make the house ready, check each room
for temperature, smooth the sheets, plump pillows,
look through every window to enjoy the various views.
The houseplants will be spruced, flowers
freshly cut and casually arranged.

The stove is warm, the smell in the sunlit kitchen
might be coffee, or rising bread, or toast
(the best smell in the home is toast) or hyacinths,
which today are a promise of Spring.
The house this Spring day is ready, every room of it.
The house is ready. Where is everybody?

Angelina Ayers

Vultures

It gets me how his bald head appears to poke
right out of the brickwork, watching me wait
for the 52. He's been watching me 30 odd years.

I waited here with Nan, pleading to pay myself on.
She tutted and pulled two pence from her glove,
pressed it into my palm. *Say please*, she said

with Polo breath, and I thought then, why vultures,
why not something pretty, canaries, nightingales.
What are you looking at, blue-eyed vulture?

Cement's made a non-migratory spectacle of you
while the rest of the 70s got torn down
and your scrutinizing me won't change anything.

At least I can leave, catch the next train out
and I will once I'm ready, a one-way to the coast.
Then we'll see, or you won't, that is. All you see's

the new builds where the Wedding Cake stood
white walls, red carpet, no aisle. 19 pounds 50
it cost to marry, no change given on the day

so a quick nip to GT News for ten Windsor Blue
and all for two years wedded. You're petrified
I'll leave you to this gritstone city, this steel mote

on the map, bloody-minded hills like knuckles
against the skyline, ready to pick off the weak.
No wonder you can't take those eyes off me.

Shifts

Back from the nursing home and locked out,
my keys with the crisps in the fruit bowl.
We don't have mobiles. No one does.
There's a phone box over on Duke Street
but where would I call? I saw my first body

this morning, she was old, of course
so no surprises. She wasn't even one of mine
but I cried to see her yellow cheeks sunk
against bone. They'd took her by twelve.
No hoist, no bed-sized lift. It wasn't funny.

You can picture how we madeshift
getting her downstairs and out the door.
But I'm sitting under the light from our block
waiting to tell you it all, how the matron
was mistaken for a patient by the driver

who ushered her into an armchair. Stowed
in the smoke hole we laughed about that
almost forgetting the death. They said
I've to get used and stop fretting, like it's just
another day. I'll be glad when you're home.

We'll talk about something else, about the night
you locked us both out, keys dropped
in the Penny Black, your shoulder barge
not up to much, and the old bloke from the flat
upstairs taking us in like abandoned puppies

or when we were meant to be out with Vinnie,
babysitter sorted, you cutting it fine in the bath
and me painting my nails huckleberry red.
You never said how it happened, mirror
smashed on the tile, your thumb sliced

like a soft-boiled egg, its bloody yolk
staining the towel. I wasn't much of a nurse
that day either, went to the shop for plasters.
You scarred under butterfly stitches, a slug
thickset and silvering. I know you've seen it

when you St Johned at Hillsborough, but she
was my first, and it must've been worse for you
but I can help now, with those dreams
you don't have, and whatever impulse it was
made that glass shatter in your hand.

If I knew where you were, I'd meet you halfway.
We could walk home, your arm slack
round my shoulder, its warm catch on my skin
stemming the thought of her sheet-wrapped face
or the thought of the early shift tomorrow.

Memphis Belle

You're singing *Danny Boy*
playing tail gunner
as we climb the ginnel
skidding the steep slew
of cobbles slippy with rain.

Your fly-by knocks me
and I pretend to mind
your Slush Puppy breath
shrugging you off,
my elbow stoking your ribcage.

I can feel the soft spaces
between your bones
the rub of clothes on your skin.
The hill can't last
and as we near the top

where you turn left and I don't,
I'm dream-slow, heavy
like skies hushed with snow.
You tease me, cheeks red
as your football shirt.

Behind me the Odeon
flood-lights the afternoon
and ahead you stand
expecting me to keep up
or at least stay close.

Elizabeth Barrett

Necklace

Lingering, not wanting to leave him –
leaving it too late and running then down *Charles Street* –
the light fading, students pulsing out in waves –

and suddenly, pouring from my body like rain,
the skitter of beads scattering from a necklace
I'd worn for two decades, rolling in the road like sweets.

I danced between the beads thinking of him
and the hands on my watch, my daughter home alone
and the steady progress of my son's school bus –

waved my hands over them, bidding goodbye to my beads
(the crowd watching the fall of my broken rosary
the grace of these *Hail Mary* feet) left them lying in the street.

I imagined him cycling by later, his wheels weaving –
thinking he'd seen those beads somewhere before,
had watched quick fingers spinning them.

That night I dreamed I stared into his eyes –
his hands unfastened knots along my spine –
I could hear sash windows rattling, a door knocking in its frame.

So I drove back next day – knelt at the side of the road
searching the gutter for the beads I had dropped,
picking through dirt and litter for what I had lost.

In Endcliffe Park

there is a gap
in a dry stone wall.
It is an imperative this gap –
if you reach it you must
go through it or turn back.

The imperative gap in the wall
is at the wedge-end of the park.
We are standing there, hesitating,
separated from my white car (openly
parked at the side of the Saturday road)
by the gap in the wall.

One of my children is with us.
We have walked the wide edges
of the isosceles park to reach this gap,
kicked and thrown the piles of dry
brown leaves he loves into the air,
watched them cascade down around his head.

We have passed the pond
for feeding ducks and throwing stones –
seen our low moans of wanting
and fear and hurt sink beyond doubt.
We have broken open and shared
our wintry, squirreled stores.

Wait for me I say to you as we stand
by the gap in the wall. *I don't know
how long it will take, but wait –
please.* You take me in your arms,
say *I love you* and step through.

Blue Moon

And if I had known –
if some winged thing had only told me
that we were not, as I thought, at the start
but the end, that the first time
would also be last – if I had known
through the slow stammer of rain
in the stolen hours of the afternoon
we spent together at the *Blue Moon*
(our secret balcony room suspended
high above the lunchtime crowds)
if I had known then that this would be
our only chance, I would have summoned
a hundred angels to our table.

Surely they would have heard the chariot
at my back – could have helped me conjure
from our words the blessing of silence,
an end to the gossip and coyness?
And then, from this urgent place,
I could have gifted this: a pack-train
of goats, laden with flowers to spread
on the table and cover our heads;
perching macaws to write you love poems
on the walls, sit on our balcony ledge;
a rope of vines to cling to – hold tight –
swing out above the chattering café
through frothing cappuccino clouds.

And then, perhaps, I would have been
brave enough for this – my tongue
along the length of your fine arms,
moving slowly across your chest; my lips
searching for the tips of your clever fingers,
discovering tenderness at the nape of your neck.
And then I could have nerved myself – let go –
have taken, astonished, my first flight –

flowers falling from my hair – or clattered
on my cloven hooves down the café stairs.
Either way, I would have heard those scarlet birds
squawk and flap as I flew, or stumbled,
out on you; have, hurrying, turned my back.

Paul Bentley

from *The Two Magicians (III)*

> *Arachnida.* This class serves more than anything else as a convenient way
> of grouping a strange assortment of creatures ... Spiders are actually of no
> economic importance.

The devil will find work for idle hands to do.
   Two boys, picking and poking for coal
on a pit tip. *It's a bad to-do.*
   The needle jumping. Mick on the fiddle
with dad. Husky, dusky, coal-black Mick.
Mixing glob with him, my hands white as milk.
He's sizing me up. Tells me what to do.
   Sees me flinch at a spider. *It's only little.*

'Bobbies', him and my dad call the police.
   A bobby in a café in town –
he's dragging out this girl by her pig-
   tails, her screams echoing all the way down.
He'd sat beside her. She'd said something.
Her dyed red hair. Dockers. Stud earrings.
Something tightening, like a vice.
   Rising towards us, looking slowly round.

Something rising towards us on the news.
   The enemy within. Coal-black Mick.
Claire's dad arrested, as little Leigh arrives,
   down at Silverwood picketing.
It took four on 'em to get him in the van
   – rest to keep t'rest o't strikers off. Everyone
in The Joker. *What I do know –*
   none on 'em were from South Yorkshire.

On their new record Johnny Marr's guitar
   on a fierce fuse. I am the sun and air

is Morrisey singing? Son and heir.
  Their benefit concert with The Fall, New Order.
Talking to grandad about it all –
God dint make men to go down an 'ole.
The news again. Johnny Marr's guitar.
  Little Leigh. The sun and the air.

Mick's big hands. Lifting bricks. Fresh air –
  whatever happens he's not going back down.
That girl's screams still echoing. Her red hair.
  Everyone in the café looking down.
Siouxie Sioux still echoing – look around
look around look around round round...
Something rising towards us, now as before.
  Up from The Joker. That bobby's hand coming down.

King Arthur striking the table
  harder, raving and growing more fierce and wild.
New Order: Because we're rebels.
  Talks breaking down. O bide, lady. bide.
Johnny Marr's guitar screaming, echoing –
mum's *Turn that down I can't hear myself think!*
Two boys on top of the pile, picking coal.
  Me thoughts I heard one calling: Child

Chorus:

*There was a women's picket arranged for Creswell ... The police were
mesmerised at first. We got up to the pit gates, then all these vans came flying
up. They tried to keep us in one spot, so we started walking up and down.
One of the inspectors was getting a bit uppity. 'You there, you say nothing'.
But this time we did say something.*

John Birtwhistle

In Fargate

In Fargate, Sheffield, where the Dutch florist
sets out his blocks of colour like a strict
field ploughed by Mondrian, a Burmese woman

stands entranced at blue water lily heads
one to a flask, in ritual array

I can taste it
        now. Mother
                used to send us

in a rowing boat
        to gather lily
                roots from the lake

I am leaning
        over the side
                plunging through

flowers to grasp
        the ever so sweet
                slippery stuff

We'd chew it before
        it ever got
                to the kitchen fire

Floating like lilies my sister and me

Playing on the Nicknames of the Registry And Council Offices in Sheffield

Notice the iron dinosaur that grabs
window, door and corridor
from the familiar *Wedding Cake*

where Sheffield couples used to make
the keys to turn in steely locks
nestling by the chill *Egg Box*.

Both of those demolished now, we
are the keepers of our vow.
This new year of our marriage I renew

all the promises I made to you.
Love, let us live attentively before
we too are grappled by the dinosaur.

In the Midst of the City we are in Woods

for Allen Capes of Rare and Racy Books

The mist this morning has a sniff of surrounding woods
of leaf mould and smouldering leaves wafted here
from hills where the autumn woods are

In a second-hand bookshop a man unwraps
woody brown mushrooms from a must of newsprint
"Too early this year," he is telling me. "Like everything is."

Matt Black

the cooling towers' farewell

two big dirty chef's hats,
risen from the Don, looking over the river,
lost behind poplars, lego-towers,
Junction 34 look-out posts,
bell-bottoms of silent power,
the colour of chinos, sand-castles,
like Cleethorpes beach risen into the sky
(and smudged with oil, smeared with toil)
looking down over Meadowhall,
we've nothing to say, nothing to say

wearing the tides, silted,
the last two pawns in a game of historical chess,
or are we King and Queen,
taller than Sheffield Town Hall,
looking down on short fat eat-your-heart-out gas towers,
twin exclamation marks,
saying nothing, knowing everything,
Mum and Dad of the steam-filled city,
knowing steam rises, and air is everything,
Bill and Ben, the Towers of Zen ...

and on one of us, black flames, pilot lights,
round the corner the faces of monkeys,
and a black rabbit looking straight over,
on the other ghosts of old castle doors,
Aztec runes of smoke and smirch, streaks,
criss-cross paths like lost civilisations,
Stonehenge for the carbon age,
we've nothing to say, nothing to say

two big birds' nests in the poetics of space,
empty cathedrals as quiet witness to the sound-track

of the endless drone-roar of the internal combustion engine,
cloud-gatherers, cardboard cut-outs,
bit-parts in the Meadowhall movie-set,
and now they can never make
King Kong And The Tinsley Cooling Towers,
muddy like the long arm of Roman Kimberworth hills
sloping down behind us,
one peeping out from behind the other,
under the skirt of motorway two stout ankles ...

and yes, we knew the names,
from when here was industry,
Edgar Allen's, Ashlow's, Howell's, George Cohen,
saw the last of Hadfield's,
where Robert Junior invented manganese steel,
the workers' boss who introduced the 8 hour day,
creator of the age of alloys,
Hadfield's, railway tracks for the world,
spitting heat and poison, sweat and bombs and shells,
pints and snap and industrial accidents, broken legs and hearts,
everything at 1100° centigrade, Union meetings, Jack and Harry,
divorces and domestics and long nights in the pub,
and the East Hecla works, emperor of foundries

till the last days, streets thronged,
pickets, police and workers, the national strike,
we've nothing to say, nothing to say,
names that ring eruptions,
Vulcan Road, Mount Hecla, fire, brimstone,
saw it all reduced to rubble,
theories of voluntary redundancy,
we've nothing to say,
and we watch as angels fall from cracks in the clouds
right into us, and steam rises, air is everything...

and here in our last nights,
we are two grim bouncers at the door to Club Sheffield,
our tops curled lips,

lonely against the purple-yellow sky,
dissolving, sad and solemn, dying for a fag,
come out here for a smoke mate,
fallen-angel gravity-clowns,
so please don't call us frigging icons,
and all those artists with something to say,
we've nothing to say,

and yes, we've seen it all,
the 60s and 70s, and 80s and 90s,
watched them building Meadowhall,
you call that cheesecake in those cafes,
we've nothing to say,
sulked through Thatcher,
nothing to say,
bit tongues over Blair, you call that Labour,
nothing to say,

looked down on Outo Kumpu,
watched the long road from the South,
the lorries lumbering up the hill,
Morrisons, Eddie Stobart, Norbert Dentressangle,
DHL Express, James Irlam, Preston's of Potto,
Wilmeda Beehive of Doncaster Coaches,
Willi Betz, the M1 of migration tracks,
seen the roads filling up
with post-industrialisation, and Polish trucks,

looking south, looking north,
by Tinsley viaduct, yes, very Meccano,
uz Tinsley towers, two huge brackets
around a 1950s tight skirt of sky,
will be gone soon,
to stalk Yorkshire like lost giants,
we will be two more missing teeth
in the steel-filled mouth of Sheffield and Rotherham,
the Tinsley molars ...

in a string across Europe, see us,
cooling tower beacons of yoga,
coil-pots, jugs of stillness,
alongside the motorways of madness,
and as opera-houses, as helter-skelters,
as two giant flower-pots for geraniums,
we've nothing to say, nothing to say,
big butterchurns, castles in the sky,
our slender waists in the wasteland of history,

and we're nearly ready to go,
a big cloud of dust and we'll be gone, move on,
see the horizon, smoother, cleaner,
and always back to Blackburn meadows,
fluted follies, Him and Hers,
in the industrial fashion parade our dark, frilly gartered thighs,
mud by twilight, never in the headlights,
glowing by Meadowhall sodium lamplight,
towers of zen, we've nothing to say,
steam rises, into the sky,
wordless, air is everything ...

Joe Caldwell

As the World Turns

Coming down today, dismantled,
Its bones packed up and shipped
To another town,
The big wheel on the precinct, the eye
You could ride for six quid and look down
On the streets, on the patchwork
Of gardens and fields,
On the valleys and towers.

In the houses, the days and the weeks,
The hands of the clocks,
The world-turning unicycles,
Painstaking waterwheels,
The minutes and hours,
The everyday lives
Of the people of the city –

They go on,
Noticing or not noticing
Its absence from the skyline.

Sharrowvale

On this street off the main drag,
Shaded by old independent shopfronts,
Resplendent in the sunshine,

The shouts from the schoolyard
Fade and recur and merge
With the hum of the distant traffic.
There is also birdsong.

The door is wooden
And clicks as it opens
With a reassuring solidity.

You are welcome.
They show you to your table.

Brick by Brick

They are rough to the touch;
Dust crumbles from the surface
Of the red rock of these bricks
With the sweep of your hand.

Step back:
See the smoothness of the structure,
The bricks connected one to one to the millions of the whole.

The weathered building stands proud
Before the glass and chrome of the new city.

Step further back:
See the tiny, determined, gradual human endeavour.

You can almost see the city being built.

Claire-Jane Carter

First journey alone over Mother Cap

If you cycle directly between two points
high on the moors
you can find the night,

though behind
the lights of Sheffield really will glitter
as you find the true height
of the hill.

The budded dark by the road
begins to batten down,
I slide through
not quite unnoticed.

Starting the descent at Froggat
the owls have joined me
for a blind, silent, skein flight.
Exalting in the gaping cold,
we skin the hill
away from the cliff.

James Caruth

Close of Play: Stannington

On the terrace of the Rose & Crown
geraniums drip red petals while wasps murmur
round the rims of empty glasses on a table
and a summer's day draws to a close.

Discarded on a bench, *The Sun* flaps open
on a picture of two young faces in desert fatigues,
blank eyes staring below the headline –
New Offensive. Allied Gains.

And I look out across the lane to a derelict field
of untended grass that runs down to tangled
boundaries of bindweed, dock and nettle.
If I was a poet, I would imagine

a bowler running in, hear the *toc*
of ball on bat, see lithe ghosts
throw down their caps to chase in hope
all the way to a white picket fence.

A breeze in the high branches of an oak
might be a ripple of applause as over Hagg Hill
clouds gather and thunder breaks miles away.
Somewhere an umpire is offering the light.

Pigeon Lofts, Penistone Road

after Stanley Cook

Above the dual-carriageway a few still cling
to the slope like abandoned crofts
of an island community long-since returned
to the world. They hide amidst the scrub

and litter, windows boarded up, doors
barely hanging on, the faded paintwork crumbling.
They are wounded by weather.

While below, the rush-hour traffic races by,
no time to consider these stately piles balanced
on the edge of decline. No one hears the wind
shake the empty perches free of bloodlines –
Ebony Giants, Blue Supremes, Janssens.
No one hears the dry flap, flap of wings
or a soft voice calling a lost one home.

Procession

For thirty minutes I have been going nowhere,
while rain falls through the overhanging trees,
rattling like stones on the bonnet of my car
as a herd of cows moves from pasture to byre.
At the city's edge life passes in slow procession.

Big as boats, their hides are white oceans
lapping black continents. The great hips
swaying in ponderous rhythm, pink udders
full to bursting. They pause to pull grass
from the ditch, with tongues thick as my arm.

At the rear, two herdsmen in clabbered boots,
flat caps pulled down over faces shiney as apples,
slap at the stragglers with salley sticks, waving
their arms as they read the sky over Lodge Moor.
Somewhere, important events are taking place.

But on this narrow lane a herd of Friesians,
their impassive eyes like pools of black water,
make a journey they have always made,
and evening settles to the pulse of a car engine,
fingers drumming on a steering wheel.

Liz Cashdan

Sheffield August 2011

Beyond the town, there's heather,
low-lying purple stretches across the hills,
blackberries ripe for the picking
in a cold end-of-August wind. And sea-less
Sheffield's holiday beach in the Peace Gardens,
with dumped sand, a helter-skelter, fountains
playing at being the sea, shivering kids
running between jets as if they were waves,
autumn taking us by stealth.

There have been no riots in Sheffield
though there's little work, steel, coal long gone,
Park Hill flats re-furbished for the rich.
We should all be protesting, in the footsteps of
Samuel Holberry, Sheffield's Chartist leader,
died in prison in 1842. I watch clouds throw
shadows over Sheffield's seaside cafes, wonder
how many people know the water cascades
round the fountain beach are named for him,
that he wanted "freedom, equality, security for all."

National Youth Theatre at Park Hill Flats: September 2011

Built way back in the late fifties, they rose high above the city
new housing for Sheffielders. Brutalism from *béton brut* –
with decks or walkways, orange, red and yellow panels.

Previously Little Chicago slums, this was to be new life
for real people in real homes. It worked for thirty years
till repairs and renovations were abandoned; problems,

problems with problem families, with problem buildings.
Now they've been sold to Splash something, a private firm
and they're going for £90,000, life-style apartments.

Last month the shell was invaded by 200 actors, moving
the action along the walkways; audience moving with them
on board this cement ship bound for a floating plastic island

where workers, conscripted into big business plastics,
had ingested plastic in word and mouth till they expired
in their shopping trolley hospital beds. And we ran

with dancing, groaning patients, down into the courtyard
till one bold youngster gave up her business boyfriend,
turned the play around, turned the workers around and

the world was saved through singing and dancing
and abseiling the heights of the apartments façade.
Players gone now, the first rich tenants will move in

and Park Hill Flats will belong to them, not us.

Sheffield Voices: 1

The ten year olds from Stradbrooke school
want to tell me about Sheffield voices.
Their grans kept the coal in the *coil oil*
but of course they have no coal now.
It'll be reight they say: and write it down
with the letter R and the figure eight.

The eleven year olds from Springfield
are learning to speak English, born too late for
di-das, the thee and thou of old time Sheffield.
At home they hear Gujerati and Urdu from
their Pakistan-born parents, Hindi from India,
Arabic from Libya, Swahili from Kenya..

The lad whose parents speak Indonesian
says his best memories of going back are
Kentucky Fried Chicken and motorways.
So that's what brings us all together.

Sheffield Voices: 2

Down Division Street, Barkers Pool, on to High Street,
voices blown in the wind, damped down in the rain.
"Big Issue, Big Issue, last three to go. Have a nice day."

There's a Moroccan market today, kelims, rugs, mats,
leather shoes and sandals, drums, curled leaf pottery,
and the smell of spicy lamb, couscous, honey and Paklava.

Last week outside the Town Hall, Sheffield Kurds crowded
to remind the rest of us they haven't got a country yet
and here are Somalis with a country they dare not live in..

I take my Spanish student friend to the Peace Gardens.
Sheffield by the sea is now Sheffield here comes the cold.
We find the names of Sheffielders engraved on the wall,

Sheffielders who died in the Spanish Civil War.
Mercedes does not know this bit of history.
She's worried about the lack of jobs in Spain.

Debjani Chatterjee

An 'Indian Summer'

September – and I see the urban fisher-folk
dreaming of salmon leaping in roaring rivers.

Sunday in Sheffield – and I walk by the canal.
The high Himalayas drum with roaring rivers.

The dragonfly flits in the Yorkshire afternoon
while Mandakini descends in roaring waters.

Once a laughing goddess roamed along these banks;
now unknown, her name resounds through roaring waters.

Ducks swim, ruffling their feathers over this landscape.
Yards away, industry storms its roaring waters.

Whatever she is called, Ganga meditates
on Summer rippling the calm of English rivers.

Note

Mandakini is the name of the River Ganges when it is said to flow in Heaven. Like the Ganges, many
English rivers too, including those in Sheffield, were worshipped as goddesses in pre-Christian times.

Sheffield Tanka

Passage to England
for a writer's life – and more.
Green dreams at eighteen.

The hallmark 'Made in Sheffield'
fiercely shines at fifty-six.

Lament for a City-Centre Hole

EEC rules filled
in Sheffield's 'Hole in the Road' –
a whole icon gone.

What I did Today

Today I blew up the Northern General – again;
bulldozed the waiting room in Hell
where I had sat all morning in a silly gown;
I strangled the arrogant GP who knew so little
but pretended to know it all;
my itching hands throttled the oncologists:
the indifferent one who cleared off on holiday,
forgetful of referring me for a Hickman Line
under anaesthesia at a half-decent hospital,
and the one who lost my consent form and thrust me
into a nightmare place of endless screams;
I fought the boffin butcher who drilled holes in me;
and finally I exterminated
every homicidal side-kick masquerading
as an angel of mercy ...
All these things and more I did today.

In violent days and everlasting nights,
I've lost count of the times I have done these things –

making not one jot of difference.

Matt Clegg

Watchers

What do you think you're doing? my wife asks
Each time I bundle our kid in a sling
And take her out, early, before the trucks
Hammer the roads. We leave the estate, walk along
The dual carriageway for a mile or so
Then cross the central reservation. Once
We surprised a brace of rabbits where weeds grow
Behind a bill-board, but never again since.

We're heading for the spot where the road cuts
Over the river. We can wait a long time
And often go un-rewarded, but it's
Worth it for the off-chance of seeing him
Slow-step the ebb and flow with such grace.
My kid is going to know what a heron is.

from *Edgelands*

Edge-lands. Showrooms, factories
Lapsing into pylon-fields.
Where the road bends, fresh debris.
A hub-cap like a felled star.
A severed tail. Grey. Still puffed.

*

Opposite the bakery,
A workshop. Smells of muffins
Percolate with scorching steel.
In the road, men in visors
Cadge lights from men in hairnets.

*

Hagg Hill Lane climbs sharply
On the turn. The inmost edge
Is cruelly scarred with welts
And divots. Not like a road,
More some cooled, volcanic flow.

*

Under a dank railway bridge,
He can't make a connection
Between a white bra and panties
And an oil-singed workman's glove.
Does he mean can't, or won't?

Night City

Starlings shuffle their flock above high-level cranes
As dusk touches the chemicals in vapour trails
Pink, then deepens them to blood. It was all like this
Yesterday and now it's barely the same. The light
      Flashes one signature
      In a million ways,
Glossing its mercury over the paintwork of
Passing taxis, flaring as headlamps strike road signs
And ranked traffic cones. Me? I'm a cog working late
In a multi-storey building at the centre
      Of town. I walk the empty
      Corridors, throwing the
Switches. I'm a small silhouette against a bar
Of light on the top floor, and I find my freedom
Here amongst details I can't control and wouldn't
Choose. Sometimes I pick up the intercom for no
      Reason, and listen to
      The voices of the street:
The hysterics of girls losing control of their

Bladders and the donkey brays of United fans
Absorbed and gone in the ambience of traffic
And herds of twenty-somethings trooping between pubs.
                    It's all here, the dreamscape
                    And libido of the
City at night, struggling to express itself
Even through wraiths like me, lost between ideas,
Virtuosos of the art of managing time.
Something happens to you in the city at night:
            At the hurting centre
            Of the bass beat, in each
Pinprick or corona of artificial light.
It's a sense of direction gone awry on
The one-way system, a sudden emptiness of
Arcades and delivery routes, or a stand-off
                    With a dead end. You can
                    Feel it aroused by the
Perfumes and pheromones of the scrum queuing for
Republic; in the thick necks of bouncers with no
Give behind their eyes. Sometimes, out of nowhere,
It hurries up to you asking for a favour
            Or the price of a meal.
            It has blood in its hair
And nowhere to go. It's in the way traffic lights
Keep on changing long after the traffic has left.

Jarvis Cocker

'Within these walls the future may be being forged'

Within these walls the future may be being forged.
Or maybe Jez is getting trashed on cider.
But when you melt you become the shape of your surroundings.
Your horizons become wider.
Don't they teach you no brains at that school?

Martin Collins

Kelham Island

I am the worn red brick of impermanence.

I don't have buildings, I boast Works.
Brooklyn, Cornish, Green Lane,
theatres of industry and craft.

They received a watery curtain call in 1864.
Now I am 'regenerated' as apartments,
housing urbanites smug with period windows.

I am the brazen legends of forgotten breweries
while a tiny building, by the sign of a fat cat,
readies the Pale Rider. The champion ale!

I am the torn stocking of the last whore
ushered out from the warehouses
to take residence in view of student halls.

I was named by the Don.
Once fuel for wheels and engines,
now witness to poetry from the Riverside.

Now those crucibles for Sheffield steel
wait lifeless by the last *Little Mester*,
his career's twilight a museum exhibit.

I am Kelham Island.
I am the worn red brick of impermanence.

Candlemass in Walkley

You can spot each participant
by the tiny conflagrations
in the suffocation
of night too soon fallen.
While they sleep,
wax gurgles with the sorrow of combustion.
Perhaps hissing at curious moths
learning caution as their final lesson
or gasping as the wind blows molten liquid
from its berth
to freeze as decoration on the earth.
At morning they run down
to praise their solar guides
and greet the long missed sun.
Its appearance may have been inevitable
but they relish the chance to fall in step
with the might of celestial movement.

Hong Kong Central Park 2010

The air is a dog's embrace.
I try to watch Tai Chi,
wonder how the aged move so fluidly,
can be synchronized and seamless,
the difference between postures,
why that woman swings a sword.

I will begin my research in Sheffield.
A man who let the Buddha take his name
will show me how to feel full body connection,
to borrow energy from the earth,
to relax my chest and demonstrate,
his frame melting like a sigh.

I will see that connection in others.
Witnessing a tea ceremony in Japan
with a love I haven't met,
she will say 'Bit long winded for a cuppa'
I will reply
'Our host feels every movement.'

Stanley Cook

Sheffield

When my father's generation were walking home,
Their bodies satisfied with work on the farm,
The greenish porcelain of evening sky
Inverted over them, Sheffield used to lie
At the other end of the single-track railway line.
They gulped up water from a bucket when they got inside
And hung their caps on nails in the kitchen door,
Striking sparks with their boots from the stone floor,
But on the living room wall were fading photos
Of men at work in smart unsuitable clothes
Whose country cousins they were. These wonderful men
For ever proved the boss was wrong again,
For ever were kept awake or sent to sleep
By a steam hammer, lodging in Weedon Street,
For ever framed in gilt hung looking down
On children being mardy or manking about;
And though the terraced houses where they lived
Make way for multi-storey flats to rise
As monuments to socialism on the hills,
Their memory is only imperfectly erased:
Works chimneys remain by which they lived to die,
Their muzzles still smoking from killing the summer sky.

Pigeon Cotes on Penistone Road

Past where a complex of multi-storey flats
Fences off the view from terraced houses
And above Weir Head where, jammed on stones,
The larger rubbish cordons off the smaller rubbish
From the lower river, a dozen pigeon cotes
Painted football colours stand in clearings
Among the willow herb. This Sunday morning

The pigeons, tethered by instinct and safe in the valley
As a match between cupped hands from the wind,
Crisscross their wings on the air. I remember my father
Fostering homers beaten down by a storm
And how my Uncle Tom was turbaned with glory
From winning the race from San Sebastian.
Sometimes to someone pigeon fanciers,
Backyard mechanics, rabbit breeders,
Hermit chrysanthemum growers on allotments
And trumpet players in silver prize bands
Are/were/will be great.

Ebenezer Elliott, the Corn Law Rhymer

Cold gropes for mercury in the thermometer ball;
No foliage remains to baffle the sun
And stone-cold statues begin to focus.
Elliott's, for example, in Weston Park,
Who bluntly states his surname to workers
Of the world he rallied with fighting words
Towards the narrow light of such a day.
Pigeons perch on him like forward children
Making up; he remains impervious
As a party leader giving autographs
On the stone soapbox of his plinth.

It was not this dog's convenience wrote the poems
But a man could be put together from passers-by,
Who once again would hear his 'Battle Song'
Unflinchingly as a bandage from his wound.
Yet a lover again and a lover of Nature
Who sat on a stone where a small stream tears the woodland
And the Rivelin rips the Pennine moors apart
Still offering unneeded water-power
To the trace of mills. Hills gather round
Where lies the preacher of the plunder'd poor,
The Ranter in his poem who preached on Shirecliffe

Before the fitted carpet of Council houses
Covered its outdoor room and oaks still waved
On Wincobank and not face-powder coloured clouds
From works below.

                Elliott's cause seems won
Now we eat untaxed our flannel slices
Of steam-baked bread: but anger remains
And days that like our souls are fiercely dark.
Not like theirs who pick their noses for faults to find
And forms of wrong for protest to practice on,
Who would almost be sorry if Jack were all right;
Like Elliott's who finding Eden abandoned
To hooligan winds that tripped its best trees up
Wrote in rhyme to Fate for explanation.

Sarah Crewe

sheffield (standard class view)

white noise
       silent howling

              birds of prey
speeding through

miles of still
       of lush of mist

a dead sheep   jackdaws
baby lambs in blue dye

trees unsure of season
ripples in landscape

loss of signal
              field fire

              this is painting
without brushes

gallery participant
static   but moving

aqua mosque
              union jack

       signs of life
boating lake

there is a city

4. meeting room (sheffield international via breslau)

no half measures
peace utopias
disarmament trickery
snake pass
sangriatic sequel

no ratfaced intentions
tea and knitting
a march into escafeld
garden of eden
blood of a rifle butt

black combat dress for
spartacus siren
from a cell

scouse elf terrorist
spotting wrynecks
in a chasm

camilla stripped bare
red rose in flotsam

does urban rapunzel
january-june

Axe Flake-Out

Left out. Pike Of Stickle boy has jag, will travel
Cousins in Thames nose dive hard drive into
Neolithic trade out, export chisel crack
To continent. A friend to a farmer
A God to a grasshopper but given the slip
Cast out collided in Escafeld drawer
If you clasp, then our curves concur
Car below would absolutely avail
Of window could shatter speed us
Back through and into gorgeous gradients
Hands out. You could give me your cracked
Street lashed palms i could soothe could heal
A valley vicissitude mine last to let light in
Nuzzled into green lush ragged ripped out
Macabre twist model of *rock paper scissors*
Tree shave suffocation scratched by crude ink sticks
Three steps from thrown out. Hold me.

Amanda Dalton

from *Mapping The Edge – a Sheffield Medea.*

1. Maddy: a beginning

My new goat dances on the tin roof and unfastens gates;
she leaves me ragged as a cabbage.
Still, each night I walk the three miles to 'The Feathers',
drag the heels of my all weather shoes,
flap flap on tarmac, *scud* along the lane.
Goat weary,

mesmerised
by every glug of water in the washing up,
the bottled clouds, the pint mugs overwhelmed by flood,
the glasses stacked like fragile towers in cities
that I saw once in a book about the future,
like a city might be now somewhere,
with roads that you can carve out with a fork,
through plates of orange sauce left over, smeared.

He came in when I was clearing tables,
clean and white and golden Nike, Adidas.
Unbreakable and sure.
His three mates and him, but just him really.
Him. I'm done for.

I'm the little pile of mash
that's on the edge of Mr Rathbone's finished plate
and he's fresh gravy, pouring over me.
I'm drowning in him, salty, comforting as soup,
except I know already he's not natural.
There's flavourings and starch in him and E621, E323, E150C.
That's bad, but much too late already.

Then Mrs Benson shouts at me to hurry

and I say, *Please, Mrs Benson...*
(think I'm going to vomit, maybe cry)
and they all hear me and they laugh and call me 'Hedges'
like she's been through one,
like birds nest in her in her you-know-where.
Then he says, Jason says, *shut up, she's all right.*
They don't laugh then.

I wish I was a hedge that hadn't just caught fire.
A still, green hedge, quite cool and safe,
enclosing goats and hedgehogs.
Ancient hedge that's made of many shrubs.
One shrub for every hundred years along a thirty metre stretch.
That's how you age a hedge.
I almost say out loud, *How old am I?*

2. Jason: an ending

I know how it looks;
I know it looks really bad
and even worse with the lad
and a second on the way,
but I tell you, Maddy was always mad,
a danger to herself, a curse.

I sometimes think I was under a spell from the start,
still am, when I wake in a sweat in the dark
just knowing I love her
and knowing I'll love her the rest of my life.
But hey, come on, get married to her?
Maddy, *my wife?*

She can't have a drink without spilling it over her chin,
she won't wear decent clothes,
she won't eat anything out of a tin,
and she actually weeps sometimes, dead loud,
cos she reckons she misses that bloody goat.

It wouldn't have worked. It was always a dodgy one.
Then Caroline comes along.
She's classy, rich, the kind of girl you know you'll settle with,
and she's willing to go to court for us to get my kids.
My mum adores her,
s'only dad, who says it's wrong as snow in August,
wrong in his gut like he's swallowed something bad.

I guess I'm sorry, yeh, I guess I'm sad
when I think how he was so made up, so set alight
that night I first took Maddy back.
My dad and scissors,
I'd been sick of the sight since I was a lad.
But Maddy, she sat at his feet like he was a king,
kept listening to his talk of forging blades
and grinding on the joint
and how to bore and tap.
Her mouth was hanging open, gob-smacked,
full of respect for every boring fact.

Then she told him how to cut a string without a blade
and how to shear a sheep.
She took the coffee table and my mother's furry rug
to demonstrate. And it got late.
And we all laughed.
And it was great.
And Dad was set alight.

Later on that night she talked about her hands and his
and her dad's hands
and what you learn and what you know inside
and what you honour and respect
and what you pass down time.

She talked about a line of blades, of cutlery,
a river made of steel,
invisible, but flowing
deep and strong through this place.

I sometimes think she came from outer space,
my Maddy.

Now my dad's not speaking what with Caroline
and her dad buying up the little cutlers' yards.
He's looking to the future,
nothing wrong with that, but my dad's took it hard.

And I'm not speaking either, I'm being hard and sharp,
clean cut, cut off from Maddy, like the best blade.
Split, divided, severed through the bone.
It's best that way.
I'm telling you, she's like her goat.
She'll find her own way out of here,
she'll head off to the hills,
to home sweet home.

Beth Davyson

Burbage

As new-builds fade to field
you bring your wine-gum mouths

up here, to spray stories over canvas edges:

bunsen burners at the neckline,
blinked-in chilli seeds,
broken vaults to the ginnel
naked mid-road sprints.

There were also, of course,
lips on unfortunate lips.

You remember these rocking in your hammocks,
pine cones glinting in the drizzle.

Russell Dobson

Sheffield, I suppose

shallow river is thick and brown
plant life edges in from the lightless echo
of banks walled with two roomed flats
new red bricks
bright, abrasive
amongst a wealth of retired factories
deep set with soot.
Fallen tree branch provides the sinister magnificence
as Skol can and split white carrier bag
catch further debris,
nest for camouflaged velveteen coot chicks,
forging a new island.

Office buildings and designer apartments
barricade the vista,
I walk street after street to pick out a chimney,
for trodden grass
through tarmac.

the corrugated wall of Wickes

an isolated row of gaunt houses
converted into a pawn brokers and a chip shop
"Go Vegan" sprawled over the boarded windows

Berlie Doherty

Leaving Walkley

Lena tries to hide her shame in smiles as
rushed by men who've come to do their job she
scuttles down the entry to the ambulance.
Her kitchen smells of urine, sour milk and
dish-cloths that have slipped behind the stove and
tea-clothes scorched from leaving over flames. She
can't cope.
Her father's photograph, his banjo, tools,
the only things she's cleaned for months,
her bath heaped with rank sheets, her
sink with dishes, fridge with
apples from the neighbours' windfalls,
garden wild with roses, and their thorns
clutch at her as she's rushed and
shaking off the hand that grabs her arm she
stoops to pull a flower-head, noticing
white mildew on the petals.
And the sudden drench of perfume brings her
down the rapid years to
yesterday, she says,
and crouches so the grass will hide
her tumbling hair and
earth as sweet as rain will
cool her skin.

Riddle Trail, Botanical Gardens

Step into the garden of surprise.
First find the place where two bright eyes
Reflect the movement of trees and skies.
An iron rose, half-open gates,
Show where a secret garden waits.

Down in the woodland of whispering green
A quiet moment to sit and dream
Now follow a dinosaur, steady and slow
To a tree that lived millions of years ago.
Mice and birds and squirrels throng
Where the spirit of nature pipes his song
Find a circle of stone opened up to the stars,
Where huge animals lived in a cage without bars.
Summer in winter, the world in one place
Outside is inside the palace of glass.
Step your way to the great stone arch
Where the riddle circle ends and starts

Pavement Poem, The Moor

Here lies
a city's heart.
There in her hills lie
her green bones, quiet under
the clutter of houses and streets.
And there in her rivers run veins
that long ago powered her mills.
Her long limbs reach to the
moors. But here, here
lies her throbbing
heart.

Jenny Donnison

Porter Brook

A house at the end of the terrace.
Small, red brick. From the front,
nothing much to it.

At the back there is a garden:
roses, foxgloves,
hollyhocks, fennel.

Bees ransack flowers.
Under trees the women sit
in patchwork light.

They drink tea or gin
from second-hand cups
of porcelain.

Over the low wall
the Porter Brook, a clear ribbon,
weaves through the city,

threading it together.
It flows over flat
stones the colours of coins.

A bridge arches the stream.
Mottled fish move
through vivid weed.

The women talk of men and herons,
glimpse turquoise-orange
iridescence.

Influx[1] (a fragment)

Benny Rothman stepped out from the suburbs
marshalled the crowd for a walk on the hill
playing his part made magic right through him
his flesh-scented conduit flooded with heat
to re-forge the deeds of the land afresh
one piece leather boots and wax jackets
swapped for grey suits in Derby assizes
peaceful trespass was his moral duty
by lawful decree sentenced time inside
marks up lines within his damp prison cell
dotted paths across plains under grey skies
soft peat retains the imprints of boot-soles
thank you Rothman we're free when we're walking
and free when we're moving over the rock
the spine and the central nerve channel floods
you snapped your loaf in half and doled it out
tore-down the signs that warned prosecution
peacefully passed where the path was open
through pressure to justify these linked-up lines
you pushed me to my logical limit
I argued these tied-up ropes as ethics
over tea these words instigated this
you said ok yes and I tomorrow
solstice auspice for rigging a system
if we get caught we'd better be civil
unlawful trespass marked on our record
for plumbing out what's hidden inside
for seeking out caverns deep in the earth
a silent serpent coiled behind the eye

1 'Here recalled is the katabasis into the Totley Tunnel's air-shaft 5, undertaken in search of the natural cavern that forms the shaft's root, the rumoured secret store of city treasures: it is sung in 672 lines in response to the shaft's vertical feet of depth; it is broken into four parts, matching the necessary four ropes tied together, the verse breaks occurring where the abseiler needed to unclip and reclip in order to cross the joining knots.'

Carol Ann Duffy

The Five Weirs Walk

I have a mother's hand and you a child's.
Hand in my hand you walk beside me now
for miles, under the cutlery silver-grey
of the clouds, the old buffed spoon
of the sun, the river Don rolling away
from Lady's Bridge, now like the rusty industrial past,
now like the blue of your future, infinite, clear.
This is the Five Weirs Walk. We are here –
and if an X were to mark the spot we'd stand
at the heart of a kiss, where change and history,
 knotweed and balsam meet. Come on then,
follow the river's narrative as the city wakes
from dreams of itself. Some walk ahead of us or behind.
I walk with you, holding the flowering bud of your hand.

William Empson

The Birth of Steel

> *(Note by Empson: This Masque for the Queen's visit to Sheffield and its University was a co-operative affair, with the plot hammered out in Committee after an initial skeleton draft by the Vice-Chancellor; additions were well supplied during my absence by the producer, Mr Peter Cheeseman, and the stage manager, Mr Alan Curtis – these additions are in italics. The music was by Dr Gilbert Kennedy.)*

The curtain rises on an Alchemist with three minions before a furnace.
He bows to the Queen.

ALCHEMIST:
Your majesty, my name is Smith,
The lordliest name to conjure with:
Iron all my family made. I'll now display
A stronger metal, a more brilliant way.
My alchemy its light on iron turns;
With phlogiston my great alembic burns,
Though unsuccessful yet, with Paracelsus' aid
Today my minions hope to forge a stronger blade,
For Zarathustra spake to me last night
In hour of Ashtaroth, by burning light
Of Erebos ... (holding up a sparkling stone)
Hic petrus
In chalybem ferrum transmutabit.
This long sought stone provides the key you seek,
'Twill change your brittle iron to nobler steel
For ancient seekers missed the way of truth
Seeking to gild their leaden crucibles
But I, with deeper learning, know that wealth
On steel, not fickle gold, must founded be,
And this existent stone, their bootless dream
To real profit turns, and does not seem
To ...
(Minion taps him on the shoulder)

MINION:
Master, two black pigeons on yon oak!
Now let it out! Now let it smoke!)
> (Crowd enters and mocks at operations with furnace)

ALCHEMIST:
Ignore the mockery of the hoi polloi;
All genius they hope, vainly, to annoy.
> (A larger magic circle is described with a whitewash brush during a
chorale)
Ut ferrum transmutarent veniunt
Cum ferro in ignem exspectant
Ut ferrum transmutarent veniunt
Cum ferro in ignem sperant.
> (Sword removed from furnace and brought forward)
The time has come to try my newforged blade;
> (A Devil appears)
Upon this anvil let it be assayed.
> (The sword smashes, the crowd laughs)
It has failed. It has failed.
> (He thumbs dismally through magic book then addresses the Queen)
> I appeal,
It is essential that I conquer steel.
Minerva, Minerva. Descend! Only Minerva now
Can save all strength, whether for sword or plough.
> (Crowd sings Hymn to Minerva as she descends)

CROWD:
Hail Minerva (etc)
> (Minerva descends in a chair and addresses the Queen after a curtsey)

MINERVA:
Royalty, I am yourself! As you would wish
I now create Sheffield
> (She fetches from her chair four white laboratory coats and a silver box.
> She distributes the coats to the minions and finally to the Alchemist)
Be you the watcher of the governing dial
– And you the pourer of the chemical phial

– You with a slide rule I invest
   To calculate, design and test.
(To the Queen, advancing to the Alchemist)
                                    This poor fish
I turn into a steel technician;
        (She turns to crowd)
And every worker to a real magician.
        (Lighting alters. Alarm clock, rack of test tubes and slide rule
        removed from box by minions. Minerva returns from her chair
        with large text-book of steel technology, stilling orchestra and
        activity of minions)
But not too fast! It is now time to look
With patience on my future serious book.
        (She places the new book on top of the old one. The Alchemist
        reads from it while minions act in accordance)

ALCHEMIST:
Massive; pearly glistening lustre;
Structure undulatingly lamellar, slaty;
In colour greenish grey to near leek green,
Slightly transparent, soft, and unctuous:
Difficultly frangible; and dense
Three times as water.
        (He turns over page)
Dodecahedral structure, with slip planes
In three oblique directions; atomic spacing
One point three six eight four ANGSTROMS.
        (Final activity to produce sword, music ending with alarm clock.
        Sword presented and Devil foiled by Minerva. She comes
        forward to address the Queen)

MINERVA: (through strings)
Majesty, as you know, we spirits are
Diffused, not distant in a star.
The real magician is two groups of men;
The hand has worked with the mind, but then
Each has got both. We need not puzzle how
They made it work: if they can do it now.
        (She returns to her chair and the final chorus begins as she ascends)

MEN:
Puddling iron, casting iron,
Is the work of this environ;
And it suits the British lion,
Puddling iron.

WOMEN:
Blending steel, rolling steel,
That's the way to get a meal,
And we're right ahead of the field,
Blending steel.

MEN:
Puddling iron, casting iron;
Send the sparks up to Orion;
Give the Goddess more to fly on;
Casting iron.

MEN AND WOMEN:
Puddling iron, blending steel;
Turn the fire on to anneal
What you feel about the siren;
Blending steel,
         puddling iron,
ROLLING STEEL.

Suzannah Evans

Thursday at the Philadelphian Working Men's Club

The pig is scandalised by the behaviour of the rabbits.
They burrow in and out as they choose, with stories
of the streets of Upperthorpe, the Tesco car park,
that close call with the Staffordshire bull terrier.
The rabbits love the duck although they think he's stupid
because he quacks like a loon at the little boy
and his father, whether they bring bread or not.

The duck has a strategy and is playing dumb.
Everyone is against the hen because she's new
with the exception of the turkey, who admires
her wit. She thinks they are all two-faced.
The Turkey is insecure and inspects his wrinkled neck
in the puddled ground. There is so much he hasn't seen.

Park Hill

Daring the drop, she swings her feet,
puts a hand to her trilby in the wind.
In neon white it says
I LOVE YOU WILL U MARRY ME.
Her name's scrubbed out
but she doesn't mind the change –

can't get sentimental about the old place.
She'll stay, ghosted among folded pigeons.
They couldn't interview her for the programme
but she heard snatches as she ducked
between flats on Gilbert Row,
watched the workmen on the scaffold.

Her mother and sister sounded distant
as the dead, voiced by the radio
and him that did it, too,
the lad with the dog
who'd picked her out, a vandal in the end,
him that made her anybody's guess.

Nell Farrell

Blessing at the Allotments

I am the one dressed for a ritual,
running shoes, iPod looped through my fleece,
mouthing the smoky prayer of a soul song.
She is simply walking the muddy paths
hands in her pockets.

The third time we cross,
something arcs between us.
We break off and smile, talk sunshine,
bird song, ramshackle sheds.
Then she says *I come here to say my rosary.*

I run on with something bestowed,
imagining *Hail Holy Queen* rising up through the trees
with the midges and the bonfires
and the broken notes
escaping from my headphones.

Every Parcel Numbered Thus

Copperplate on an old map in the library
records that *every parcel is numbered thus.*

The green wooded edge where we garden
once farmland, now smaller plots

gifts of land for those who won't inherit.
We are number 62 or twelve years here

or thirty yards by ten. The library tells us little else
but history for allotments is the chemistry of soil

a hand cupped round a breath of seed,
the jars of marrow chutney, plum and apple jam.

And the old man with his dog that afternoon
who crowded out the quiet lanes for me

wheelbarrow traffic, war-time gardeners
digging through the daylight-saving nights.

Look

Someone has carved into the rubber window frame
by the back seat of this bus.
Not incised initials or graffiti
but a craftsman's grain of liquorice stripes.

Maybe the sunshine softened it
and they couldn't help but
delve into a bag or pocket
for a comb or chisel
a credit card or library book

to dig and spread and swirl and scrape
until it dripped like Dali's clocks
aniseed and dark molasses melting
into unexpected labia
blackcurrant wine gums
and the worn down soles of shoes.

How could they bear to leave it?
Did they note the number of the bus
and roam the city desolate and cold
as all the wrong and empty galleons passed them by?

Veronica Fibisan

The Joint Snake

The child is playing with a joint snake
he leaves it on the ground
it catches roots.

On Cornish Street, just on the left
the third gate boasts
'Enquiries at time office',
as if they sold tickets to the past.

No tax machine, the window open,
a flaking scale on the discarded skin of Jormungand,
ready to shine again on a new body.
Inside: 'Office Enquiries. Ring'
the button is long silent
through a guttural passageway.

A wide wooden wheel rests against the wall
like a lopsided tooth, a cavity in the middle,
lamps hang religiously from
the beams, like earrings.
A patch of cloud opens up into a pearlescent bandaged wound.
The cutlers' wheel is sharpening time's claws
in rusty finish.
Hooks on chains, a web undangling in the drafts.
A flood smudge on the wall,
is stretching itself into a baby snake.
Jaffar, fighting a battle against time,
there are just bits and pieces of a Rubik's cube nobody can solve.
Jonah is in the giant belly of the fish
more like a snake, a need to escape.
Pulled out the tooth on my way out.
The factory has shed its skin and moved on.

Roy Fisher

They Come Home

To win back the parents
from the passage-laws;
bring them home together,
bury them under a tree;

spread their bone-dust,
that now stares back at the sun
for the first time and not for long,
two colours of dry limestone,
female and male,
met for the first time, your
fingers and mine mixing your dead
in a layer across the topsoil,
set with corms,
aconite and crocus,
directly under a double-winged
trapdoor of live turf;

by no means separate the dead
from anything.

To have them
won back, by awkward custom;
lifted free
of the crematorium counter
and out from the poor
vestige of common ceremony;

left to our own devices, holding them,
each in a stout paper bag that
covers a squarefaced container
of dull plastic, coloured like
milky cocoa, with a toning beige lid.

And the last journey of all, of necessity
by way of the car-exhaust workshop;

they travel, your foot steadying them upright,
together on the floor, concentrated,
come down to owl-size in their jars,

and they stay there for an hour without us,
lifted up high on the greased, shining
hydraulic pillars under the workshop roof-lights,
closed in my grey-green car
while its rusted and burnt-out piping gets
yanked off and replaced. They come home
over a new smell of hot metal.

By no means separate
from anything at all.

Jars and their paper bags,
name-labels,
go to the bin, with the clearings-out
from the discontinued kitchen;

each has still
a whisper of human dust that
clings to the plastic,
the boundary a mad
regress beyond the microscopic.

They're going again in a day or two:

to be in part twice-burned
in city flames; eight hundred
degrees of the lance-burner
under the oven's
brick arch, and then whatever
blast of the municipality
lifts the remainder haze clear of Sheffield
and over the North Sea.

Leah Fleetwood

In the Botanical Gardens, Watching Solomon

The Gardens empty now of strollers, and fill
with shadow soft as that dove's throat.
The lawns smooth to chamois, the air strokes.
Yet through this gentling, peonies blaze,
bloodbursts of silk, and raise a hunger
for the marking of all kinds of beauty.

In the emptying Gardens, a small boy remains,
as intent on his steps as a high-wire walker
crossing between pinnacles above a sheer ravine.
The squat, foot-high wall from which he must not fall
circles a monument to the dead of Crimea.
The frown in the stepper's dark eyes reveals joy.

In the darkening silken air, his solid mother stands
as if tranquillized by twilight, and I think
I see her let go the furrows between her brows,
see her soften, as the stone monument softens,
see her radiate a gentling rosy inner sun.
The dove's breast cascades, but slowly.

Cu-cooh-cu ...

Your ma, little lad, tells me you live at the top
of a high-rise, and every evening you drag
her here (as the evening Gardens turn to silk
and gleam). Every day, she says, you cough
and cough, scratch at eczema, scratch and cough.
Trinidad rain, she says, is always warm.

So this is your refuge, child, and I wonder
if you see me as an alien invading your space.
Do we distract you as your mother and I

talk about you, and about the loss we share
of the sight and smell of crops ripening;
of rain that heals; sharp stars; foraging hen?

Say goodbye to the lady, Solomon. No, don't
force him to break his own spell. I wave:
Goodnight, Solomon. His silence is hard.
I turn towards my exit onto a raucous road.
Bye-bye, lady. I see you, I see you soon. Soon.
Sleep well, Solomon. Sleep well, sleep well.

Cu-cooh-cu ...

Seen From A Bus

In the Peace Gardens a man stands, one hand
    holding out a white plastic carrier,
the other fishing, fishing in a greenish pocket.

Starlings soar, wheel, touch down, rehearsing
    the dressage of that long flight,
star-programmed to survive and thrive.

Beyond the Town Hall comes the edge of weather
    from Iceland; in the Gardens still,
the man fumbles, fumbles, turning the colour of dusk.

Sunday Morning, City Centre

Foetus-wise, the man lies,
as if the pavement's his private beach,
his head not cushioned from concrete
by so much as the sodden bulk
of the city's weekly Property Guide.

On her way to Meeting, Ms Tyne blinks.
When this poor chap keeled over,
had a diet of rough drink and fag-ends
eaten away his sense of direction?
Was it despair that buckled his knees?

Too close to her toe, a dead bottle rolls ...
Ah but, she thinks, should this sack of offal
actually be the Son of Man, testing,
she must look into his eyes – *remarkable* eyes –
and see the Inner Light of Creation.

But this man, coiled in his stink,
awards the seeker a slow slow *wink*,
and follows it, as careless she bends closer,
with an obscenity wrapped in a twisted grin,
blind to her sisterhood, alert to her gender.

His odour is ripe, his habits of mind too,
but of the fresh of this day she's taken a swig.
So, faster than thought, she ... *winks* him back,
winks him as strong as neat tea. The sky in his eyes,
Ms Tyne notes, is blue and larksome, or *brazen*.

An inspector of buses approaches their space,
and to whiskers and uniform she refers the case,
and leaves the fallen one in his rank puddle
of sunlight, spittle, his and a tomcat's pee,
and last night's depressing excesses.

As Cathedral bells change to one-note tolling,
and the Meetinghouse heating roars, then is quiet,
among the circled sitters, silence gathers.
Soup to give them heart warms on the stove,
snowdrops on the table help them think of spring.

But now another element of peace comes to fall,
like a shawl around shoulders, as a dazzle

of thick-thronging snow illumines the windows.
In the High Street a mound stirs ... laughs ... curses.
A police van quits its brief sirening and brakes.

And Ms Tyne – often, she'd say, a drifter herself –
is comforted by the man's imminent rescue;
he will now, she is sure, be overcoated and fed.
Worrying, though, is her slowness to solemnify
her glad eye, and to undo the winks exchanged.

Cliff Forshaw

The Netherthorpe Parrots

Woke to squawks.

Up here making coffee
(Friday), looked down to see
a carnival of parrots, parakeets?

Birds of Paradise for all I know,
screeching in our sickly
municipally communal tree.

Bags, wrappers, fast-food trays
caught in branches. (Storms the other day.)
Looking down from the walkway,

saw the reds, blues, yellows, greens
of maybe a dozen different species
calling the odds in that bird-quick tree.

Three old dears with shopping wheelers
stopped to chat with two old wheezing geezers.
Echoes followed me down the reeking stairwell.

Friday. FUCK. Shazza. BNP.
No one in Planning believed my story
of the gaudy, bird-mad tree.

Later, Maria-Angeles,
– new temp from the Agency –
slid me the freesheet, picked up at the station;

circled, how that week's storms
had hit some Peak District stately pile,
destroyed outbuildings. Highlighted,

including an aviary.
Not too late to hope, I hope,
for some kind of augury

     (Keep. Ruled and ripped along the crease.
      Fold into inside pocket.
      Catch her big brown eyes.)

in how those brightly awkward visitants
had fled that Lord's estate for mine.

Friday.

Andrew Forster

Brothers

Saddled with you for the afternoon, me and Paul
ambled across the threadbare field to the bus-stop,
talking over Sheffield Wednesday's chances in the cup
while you skipped beside us in your ridiculous tank-top,
spouting six-year-old views on Rotherham United.

Suddenly you froze, said you hadn't any bus fare.
I sighed, said you should go and ask Mum
and while you windmilled home I looked at Paul.
His smile, like mine, said I was nine and he was ten
and we must stroll the town, doing what grown-ups do.

As a bus crested the hill we chased Olympic Gold.
Looking back I saw you spring towards the gate,
your hand holding out what must have been a coin.
I ran on, unable to close the distance I'd set in motion.

Wheels of Steel

In this town where horizons are close
the bus labours past cooling towers
and along Sheffield Road, stopping
by mills and forges for soot-stained workers
who sit up front and leaf through *The Sun*.
We're at the back, reeking of patchouli oil
and reciting band names like credentials.

In the city, we march through the Hole in the Road,
a bomb crater they built the road around,
making the best of things: a subway,
a hub with exit routes like spokes,
roof-less, open to the chalky night;

straight up Fargate to gather like pilgrims
on the City Hall steps, wait for doors to open.

A full house for Saxon, local boys made good.
Waves of chatter are swept into a roar
as houselights dim and guitar chords slam
with the rhythm of hammers on iron.
Beneath the emblem of an eagle, Biff Byford
sings *Never Surrender*, sings of motorcycles,
cars, trains, planes: of ways of escape.

Badlands

> *It's the working, the working, just the working life*
> Bruce Springsteen, *Factory*

He was singing of New Jersey, not South Yorkshire
but cooling towers coughed smoke into skies
above our town too. There was no darkness
on the edge of town, with no break between towns
held together by factories in a chain of light.

There were no boardwalks to strut but Fridays
workers washed away the grime and dressed
to wring some pleasure from the working week.
Sixth formers, we stayed in corners, but George
was punched because someone didn't like his shirt.

We were promised University, an exit
and the music was our passport: that voice
like a furnace roar, a thundering pace
that could burst through any barrier,
the words we repeated like a mantra.

Neil and Cathy looked set for easy passage
then she became pregnant, they got married

and he signed on at British Steel, not long
before it was broken up. I thought of them
when I last heard Bruce. Unlike the song

no-one would have swum in our river
but I wonder if they ever drove out
to Ladybower, in search of green space
and stared at the water for a glimpse of
the Church Steeple, last sign of the drowned village.

Michael Glover

To the Moor

> *a toast to its coming resurrection*
> *as the shoppers' paradise*

Down this gently sloping street,
Down this mecca of old-fashioned shopping pleasures,
Let my feet go tripping and skipping.
Let old shillings jangle in my pocket
And new notes come spilling.

Let me say those names over to myself –
Pauldons, Atkinsons, Roberts, Redgates –
As I dart into first one and then another, ever singing.
Oh glorious palaces of bygone enchantment,
You who hold out to me forever
Promises of new coats, and ever sheerer stockings!

And when I mount the bus back, weary, to Pitsmoor,
Laden like a mule with bags in abundance –
Too many to be carried, yet still I carry them –
Toys for the kiddies, a new coat for mother,
A trilby for father...

I ask you, O Moor ever more-ish,
To stay vivid in my heart and my mind forever.
(And forgive us, o furious father, for the damage to the pocket.)

Back Yard Scene, 45 Coningsby Road,
Fir Vale, Sheffield 1958

My mother ran and whisked the washing in.
The soot flakes fell, black snow from a grey sky.
The beer barrels came trundling along,

With surly men in aprons by their side.

The shelter that had kept the Germans out
Stood staunch and ugly by the lavvy doors.
We crept in there to hear our voices shout
Out swear words, tell real ghost stories, lose balls.

An outside lavvy's not a bad thing though,
Especially when the greens make you feel sick.
I stuffed them in my cheeks like hamsters do,
And shot them out in bits. The water flicked.

Roe Woods, Sheffield 5

It is likely to be here once again that I find you.
This is the spot where you would always be sitting,
Shoeless, arm carelessly thrown back, peering idly
    into some clump of bushes.
We shared the pleasures of this drifting woodland.

It is likely to be tomorrow that I shall chance upon you.
You were always waiting for me tomorrow, then tomorrow,
    ever ready to give me your signal.
It was always a smile that you gave me, barely noticeable,
And yet I saw it, at no matter what a distance
    I might happen to be standing.

It is always here that I shall remember you.
It is raining today, adding some weight to my shoulders.
I lick at the drops with my tongue's tip, I smile,
    and I idle.
I am, as ever, expectant for you. There is no one here
    to prevent you.

English Teacher walking up Barnsley Road, 1967

A stony, bookish man. A life apart
From all the other lives along that street.
A man in a black coat in summertime.
A man pernickety with single leaves.

A stary, bookish man, sparing of words.
A man who nodded when he thought to nod.
At other times, some studied sideways glance
At walls, flowers, trees. Or inward, to some god.

A bookish man, unneighbourly, tall, dour,
Who let his washing hang there, rain or shine.
A man forever walking through these parts,
Swinging a leather bag, shapeless with age.

Sally Goldsmith

Heeley

Don't know who built this terrace –
some company out to make a fast buck
when the railway came and men were needed
to feed Skeltons' Tools and Hardy Patent Picks.
I don't know who lived here then, when
there were no bathrooms, only tidemarks,
chimneys coughed and you couldn't see
the hills at the end of the street,
when there were no cars parked nose to bumper,
just kids running down jennels into back yards
where they must have tried to grow
a few spuds in earth that hardly saw the sun
and getting caught short in the night
meant a long walk across next door's yard
in the dark; damp newspaper on a nail.
I don't know if the ashes seeded in our garden
came from trees softening this valley
before the railway, the houses, Hardy Patent Picks.
Black bricked corners croak out the names:
Rushdale, Oak Street, Shirebrook Road.

Received Pronunciation

As a boy, my Sussex granddad could
spot the runty dillin in a pig's litter,
play the fool down the pleached twittern,
cry fainits when he wanted out of the game,
make jokes about the daglets on a sheep's bum
comparing them to his own number two's.

From the Warwickshire lot I got
the blart of waltzers at Stratford Mop,

learned to swill the sink after washing up,
call down the jutty at the side of the 'us –
loud enough to wake the diddikais about whom
my mother said I never should.

In rural Oxfordshire, I wuz moi duck
to aunts who let me tiffle biddy hens
off their eggs, bring in pecked bottles
of miwk off of the step, nudged me
out of looking a sawney, warned me
to avoid the bunt of boys or even a cow.

In Sheffield now with you, flower,
I look after us tranklements, crozzle
me bacon and modge me pudding,
put t' door on t' sneck, go to t' foot
of our stairs, let da into t' entry, talk
clarty at neet, laik and love da till ah dee.

Relish

'Endo's of Leaveygreave
doin' business even now
still darkly brown
no anchovies
no capers but plenty of spirit
an orange waistcoat and a neat flat cap

just the stuff
(nothing fancy mind)
for a slosh on your corned beef 'ash
your once-upon-a-time Butler's meat and potato

Fairytale

Up on the Houndkirk Road
in a foxy coat and pixie hat
with goosey snow deep enough to dream in,
a dripping sun on distant towers sparks
the edge of a corporate world
where the reds might come in the night
and jolly socialist santas bring
new mornings for all the boys and girls,
even the bad girls in their foxy coats
up on the Houndkirk Road.

Cora Greenhill

Seen in Sheffield, Summer 2011

This is what boys are for! To strip
to the hip-sagging baggy pants;
shrug, slouch; then somersault to the brim
of the fountain; cat crawl the wall,
cartwheel, lazy-vault a stone plinth,
bend knees and flat foot it free-style
down the stepped seven levels
of stone sliced by blades of water.

This is what boys do: brace
on the handrail of city steps, spring
so that two feet lunge up to stand
on the next rail. Let go, drop, land
squarely in size 12s on the pavement.
Stroll back to the crowd, unflinching,
unsmiling, like no one's watching. Cool
as this cutting edge curve of water on steel.

This is what public sculpture's for: to mirror
these moves. This is what public spaces are for.
This is what Saturday afternoon's for:
sliding down banisters on one hip,
September not quite here. This
is what boys are: poems freed in air
in Sheaf Square among the sandwich wrappers,
breakfalling among pigeons.

Alan Halsey

Mutability Cento: a cacophony for 10 or more voices

still no idea where it was exactly
round the corner from Tudor Square
the paste land later than Ruskin's time
from when it was the Naughty Girls' Home
That our daughters may be as corner stones
the picture wouldn't help you to recognise
only 2 months later
the best view is if you go up somebody's steps
a little way from Bell Hagg Road
it was a tragedy they shoe-horned
it into a Millennium box
      how many and where
      the public toilets used to be
      I can recall Fitzalan Square
      glazed roof and fancy tiling
      Surrey Street with goldfish in the cisterns
      Moorhead (not sure)
a long shaft revolved close to the ceiling
on the third or fourth floor which diverted
the power by a drive belt to the buffing machines
I think it was called Cadman Lane
it shows the Electric Light Works on the map but that
was the factory opposite I was mixing it up with
there was a quadrangle and Housing used the front part
they called the Manager the ghost because
he glided in and out and he mumbled
so posh that no-one understood
      and next to the library at Highfields
      some on the corner of London Road & Queens Road
      at the junction of Cemetery Road & Sharrow Lane
      one Top of Toyne Street Crookes
Where did Pearl Street go
before someone put ashes down

Pearl Street was great sledging
one of the girls that lived near the gennel
tried to get us talking Dog Latin
I went round to sweaty Betty's
on the corner of Priory Road
      one on Bramall Lane
      one for men only just up the road from the Wicker
      the one opposite the Hallamshire
      a nice little cottage turned into a cafe
      also a sarnie shop at Crosspool
      by the Cemetery entrance
a staircase took you up on the roof overlooking the river
at tempered springs at warren street on heavy springs
the building's still there but the company's gone
zoom in on the sign and you'll get the picture
the writing's bad hard to read
what's left of it's a body parlour right on effingham street
ted phoenix was a fitter there and tinny joe hell
and the Little Sisters of the Poor
allowed in on the shop floor
      gents next to the Broadfield
      up for rent as a kiosk
      and next to the White lion
      part of the train station
      sat atop that wall
no it's not the right place
the right place is 50 or 60 yards further down
and about 30 feet upwards where the brick walls are
but that isn't where Mulligan's Mansions was
someone told me the doorway on the other side
was the entrance to Heeley Station
a long dark tunnel with three offshot ramps
most likely where an old City used to be
the mortar's only one layer thick
something to do with the drain pipes
as there's two enormous valves
      ladies and gent at Hillsbrough
      now part of Mr Tse's restuant

or something like that
and what about the ones
perched over the Sheaf
where it joins the Don
the santas grotto with a row of fountains
lit up at the bottom of the moor
when it went from london road to leopold street
an old bomb site before the Manpower building
market stalls there on market days
you had to go through a kind of maze made of picket fencing
to where the lorry parked up for the Polio injections
huge queue waiting to be stabbed by the man with the blunt needle
one on Commonside
another on Heavygate Road
structures still there but bricked up
also underground ones down Dixon Road
near the Rag & Tag
a small shooting gallery with two 35mm cinema projectors
on the left as you went in
I'd cut up a side street from Abbeydale Road
a steep shortcut from the rickety bridge across from Heeley Baths
near a Temperance Bar that sold good Sarsaparilla
a proper snug
wood panels and pumps
that was Tony di Donno's
Blonk Street bridge bricked up
Bridge Street bus station
the Hole in the Road
as always full as it was smelly
that's sure to bring up Pond Street Nora
I heard she ran off with the Duke of Darnall
who directed traffic in his frock coat and spats
he wasn't deaf and dumb when Big Albert moved him on
Nora had a child in the change and it was taken off her
she ate all the heads off the tulips
the policeman I don't think it was Albert
it could have been Popeye
said he wouldn't piss on her if she was on fire

Alan Halsey   99

Mushroom Lane at the side of Weston Park
some at sheffield lane top now a cafe
the little gem at Nethergreen
with the burnt orange curved glazed bricks
one in Archer Road
someone said she'd love to rebuild
as a garden folly
the buses revved their engines from about ten past eleven
nothing worse than a non-starter at that time of night
then the insects
inspectors blew their whistles
Acme Thunderers five minutes later
we were always in the tingalary track
Commercial Street to you
Comical to me
they liked to be first off the grid
and beat the lights before the whistle
       The loggia-style one on Ecclesall Rd South
       one on wellington street
       and garden street near the old drinking fountain
where's the You Are Here map gone
when you pressed the buttons little bulbs lit up
showing where places were
a contortionist could lean on them all
there were always some that didn't work
       one made of green slate (gents)
       in the middle of Meadow Street
       the Ringinglow ones
       now a Rocking Horse Shop
the whale was in a glass fronted case
long dangly things in its mouth
it was dead and they were moving
it round on the back of an artic
it was someone near Ponsfords
I meant somewhere
       on the left at the traffic lights on Rutland Road
       the remains of a Gents only
Wrong road never wrong
       High Green had one at the corner of the park

Geoff Hattersley

Untitled, South Yorkshire, Mid-Eighties

When we get to the Wop
the bar staff are mopping up blood
and though it's only twenty past ten
the shits won't sell us a drink.
Except for a few hairies
clinging to pint glasses by the juke-box
the place is empty anyway.
It seems some smartarse in a suit
looked at one of the Angels
the wrong way, so they held him down
on the floor by the bar
(where the bar staff are now mopping)
and removed all his teeth –
'With a pair of pliers, and no
anaesthetic,' says the landlord.
We talk him into selling us
a Guinness carry-out, he's not
too bad a bloke. Motorhead
have been in town, their fans
are all over the place
and on the train, grunting like apes.
One of them tosses off in the aisle,
looking up at the security camera
till someone else pulls it down
and starts a game of rugby with it.
Everyone is laughing.
A man with a glass eye
sits down next to me and tells me
I'm Nigel Fisher, child murderer
just out, and John turns round
and asks if he wants his eyes
to match. He looks
sort of startled, moves to another seat –

runs like scalded bear
when he sees us getting off behind him
in Wombwell. Some miners
have overturned a police car
outside the Prince of Wales
and kicked the coppers unconscious.
Coppers are everywhere,
assaulting just about anybody.

Gratuitous

It was raining, my shoes leaked.
I was hawking poetry magazines
and some very distinctive
wallpaper catalogues.

In Rare 'n' Racy I exhumed
three grimy *Urbane Gorilla*s:
'Six years old and twenty
out of date,' I quipped.

The bookseller led me
to the autographed copy
of *The Tin Drum*, First Edition,
locked securely in a glass cabinet.

It would have been
good to turn its pages,
to feel its
weight in my hands.

Christmas Shopping
You were writing dud cheques
like no one's business,
I was splashing
the forged tenners around.

In the hole in the road
someone sang
'Take Me to Tulsa',
snow settling on his sombrero.
I tossed him a tenner
screwed into a ball.

A woman approached
armed with documents
and truth;
she was selling badges,
a definite bargain
at a tenner apiece.

I signed the petition
to end the war,
I do a lot
of possibly useless writing.

Jeanette Hattersley

Mazeppa's Men

Mazeppa Chambers sounds like a big name
in music, celebrating little men
in big fires all along the railway lines

into Sheffield, before the sheds emptied
and purple spears of weeds gathered
closer than workers at Union meetings.

Mazeppa. She could sing of the sorrows
of slingers, the troubles of lathe-turners.
From labourer to foreman, everyone

could get into her act. She could sing of
a bare blue skyline, of houses for sale,
of men smoking on benches in the square.

Mazeppa Chambers. Men idle around
that cold building, the still grey carvings
of craftsmen on the walls. Mazeppa's men.

Off The Track

Four years of awkward bus routes and cement mixers
for this: restaurant specials and a new brand of beer,
white-gloved majorettes marching through the streets,
a stadium with more light bulbs than Las Vegas.

Those on main roads have been fortunate, their houses
getting the full treatment. See the gloss of new roofs
as you climb east, the plaster, smooth as royal icing,
the butterscotch of sandblasted stone. Hear the roar

without the TV as you stand in your back yard,
five miles from the race, wrong side of the starting line
where pipes rust, walls crack, darts trophies tarnish on sills
and a souvenir balloon hangs limp from a rail.

Tarmac On Roses

The children like it best when we turn off
at St Saviour's Roll-End Centre,

its plated windows giant steam-irons
the bluebottle eye of a meshed oval.

They play games: Hold your breath until
the flats on Grandad's allotments.

A yard with no school, *Mick's Motors,*
To The Glory of God and Ford Escort

on the wall, *Krypton Tuning*
and the massed mouths of tyres, hanging.

They always laughed at Bathroom Bonanza.
I was christened there

before the one-way system. Olden days,
the children say, dirty babies.

I know by heart their jokes,
this silence heavy as tarmac on roses

at the house I will never return to,
the blinds empty as ruled feint.

Lewis Haubus

Leaves Or Breath

Beside thatched roofs and bandstands donated in 1905
the bowling green slept like a naked board game.
Its customs sucked away through morning and frost.
From an October bench, determined wood ring veins
creased against key carved names
before retiring to the blistered ulcers of surrendered leaves.

Between them repressed roll ups splintered like teeth
and a Simian nonchalance changed this seat
from a place where men huddled in life boats
to a glassy, sniggering mouth.

Eternal as a tongued cut pulsed
Josh lovez Beth. As if something was seen
in the patrolled eyes of comrades lost in quiet game.
A spark that burned from your gums until you took the marker
with ferocious hands and wrote something, anything
that felt like it deserved to last longer than leaves
or breath.

Collapse

In the refining process for neutral spaces
eyes search out the moment
where sky ends and smoke begins.
They pore over broken roofs and spaces in slab,
they stagger onto the Don,
hang like heat,
and browse the gift-shops at the end of history.

Cracked glass piles up like paint,
it floats behind no parking signs and prevents pausing

before the worn-out clock that is always three forty.
The weathervane never changes, though today feels like a furnace,
or a leak in a dam that was filled only once.
A plaque sticks to the walls locating a lost cellar,
finding more hollow brick.

Islands wait with the patience of rain
for the insurance claim of a Victorian age.
Barricaded beneath remembering
lives sputter into industry.
As the hotel closes its doors from outside
walking sticks spit and trill against pavement.
Two passing gentlemen raise their hats.

Soot stuck to a mirror
would tell that on these shell-like streets
workers sparked off each other,
that window frames made out of matches
looked over submerged settlements,
and that you renew
the lease on the plot you will never own.

Ray Hearne

from *Songs of Robert the Cutler*

all talk

from the darkest hull of the head
from the cold light of day's contradictions
from the high hill's rhythming contours
from the dull earth's heaviest ores
from the loud mouth of the forge
from the brazier's fiery barrenness
from the charcoal's black heart
from the flames' transfigurative lips
from the crucible brimming with speech
from the smoke's vernacular chaos
the maker divines and conjures, lures
from dross, its vestigial urge to prophesy
from metals their consent
from lead's inertia, its shapeless inclination to escape
from iron's reticence, its epics
from mute alloy, its murmur and ballad
from silver's silence, its definitive song
from the self-absorption of gold, its gushing circumlocutions

Beyond

At the back of Mary Flynn's cottage, that hurling field.
Me and our Kid exchanging Parkgate muck
in our lungs for the ruder scents of green; untold
rural lushness; a music of hurl upon puck,

the hell for leather tumult of ash against ash.
Our vigil, the Parish lads' nightly practice matches;
spirits of ancient Gaels made local flesh;
goal-posts at either end like our dropped aitches.

That thistly plot behind her house, and Dad
showing us the basics, brand new hurls in our hands
pelting at stones, we drove him quickly mad
skying them over ditches onto neighbouring farmlands.

Before we left for the boat he bought us shirts,
champion Kilkenny's immortal black and amber,
straight and narrow stripes lining our hearts
good and proper with high hopes beyond number.

Knocktopher; Kilmoganny; mythical acres
walked for years across our living room;
an Irish Tyke, I sported in Woolworths sneakers,
one foot pointing home, one home from home.

Outside the Sheffield Tap 2011

What is it can characterise these mealy-mouthed times?

'Austerity' trips without irony from familiar lips
Like 'he's behind yer!' chants at pantomimes

The same old smirkers' re-upholstered crimes
Have bolstered the spring in that step, the jut of those hips
The swagger of the nipped-and-tucked-to-the-silicon-pips

Barely half-seven, yet somewhere a midnight chimes
Cinderella and Jack have missed their call

Here, the football-shirted are well on the ball
Savouring beers, a remnant of burger and chips

Others caught napping, doze through their own eclipse

Songs collapse into hand-clapped kop-choir rhymes

And a poem without legs can only crawl
Up the side of a university wall

Rob Hindle

Princess Street to the Wicker, April 1925

> *The journey made by members of the Park Brigade, a notorious gang,*
> *following the murder of a soldier.*

There is work going on in the English Pewter Company,
knocking and whirring through the windows, a radio.
On the bridge, green is spouting, nettles and ferns –
there must be rain trapped in the mortar, drip feeding
tap roots, each train's quake slaking the filaments.
The river shudders, ripples like milk skin.

This is where they found mixing chromium with steel
stopped the steel corroding. 1913, all the world mustering
arms, a knife's edge. You could throw it in the river,
it would still be there, flashing in the stones like a fish.
In Princess Street, the arches bricked in, windows blackened,
these last terrace houses are shiftless and feral.

They said the blade that killed Jock Plommer was a bayonet
kept in a black case, elbow to fingertip long. As he sits dying
in his doorway and his wife not touching or looking
at the dark wet pooling on her step, faces come with a light,
with their bits of story, the bottles and razors, the lead
and steel of the Park Brigade men, seven or ten of them.

They hit him on the head with a bottle.
They hit him on the head with a child's scooter.

From the corner you could go anywhere, Leveson Street,
Warren Street, under the arches of Norfolk Bridge, over the river,
its yellow silt, a white duck dabbing in the chiaroscuro.
Here is a tossing ring under the arches, the ha'pennies spinning
over men's heads. In the dusk the pikers watch for the cops.
Whistle as the coins drop, watch them scatter.

In the event of any road vehicle striking this bridge

Between the white van pulling up and the BMW pulling away
there is nothing but the wide, pale urban sweep of Attercliffe Road,
its flat curve featureless as a hinterland. It has outgrown
the river with its births and deaths, its awkward stinks and noises.
In the cool glaze of a showroom, a red Ferrari and a blue Porsche
occupy their exact spaces. Exhilaration, seduction and power

says the sign, vehicles to stir your soul. There's not a soul about.
The Park boys swagger towards town with blood on their hands.
United have just won the FA Cup and the pubs are full of it.
As they come past the gates of Albion Works, their faces
twilit and pale, you can hear their swearing right down Saville Street.
In the gun-green glass of Saville House I am a silhouette, a trace.

You have the right not to remain silent

PC Hogan puts his notebook away, hand pinched from scrawling
names and weapons. The victim is hauled to the ambulance,
people at every door. Lol Fowler, Wilfred Fowler, George Wills,
Amos Stewart: they know the names better than United's eleven.
The road slows into the Wicker arch, its bus-lit shadows.
Here is transience and lycanthropy, somewhere to get lost.

They have put benches here, but no-one settles or waits.
The Station Hotel's the key, Commercial Accommodation,
dinner at the bar, the windows to the street grimy, back rooms
looking at nothing, brick and washing. There are no longer
trains to Manchester, but even the weed strewn line curves away.
A green cross outside the pharmacy flickers, entranced, entropic.

Bottles in bags and in crates, empties.
A substation: *Danger of death*

This was called Bridgehouses, low-rent shanty below the town,
the river turning round it and under it. In flood the water surges
right down the street, filling cellar after cellar with black stink.

Nothing is here forever. In The Big Gun, in the Bull and Oak,
no-one flinches, even when a glass is smashed on the bar,
even when a man goes down, face in his bloody fingers.
Between the Bull and the river once, the shambles, raw butchery
with its reek and swill. This is where they got them, the Park gang,
slashing and fighting, blood and spit and snot. The river is hissing
under Lady's Bridge where the road ends and the town begins,
where the castle was and now the market, its pet shop smell
and café fluorescence. Everything must go, the river goes.

Jenny Hockey

Writing at Large

Squeezed between 4x4s, my Skoda waits
in the John Lewis car park
where gaps fit only slimmer cars.
Crabwise, I get back in, see
through windscreen grime
the cleaned spaces of TOSSER,
tracing the passage of a coarse thumb,
someone over-burdened with body,
whose insult I dirty back over
with pay-and-display slips scrunched for re-use.

             ***

Ginger and alive with wind,
trees talk over my head, fire and water-tongued
by turn, scatter leaves that heap
scarlet and orange among our denim drab,
while the bus, droning its own cycles,
beams tangerine, foliage bright,
83 BENTS GREEN.

             ***

A low building watches
behind the roadside bench,
as buses stop-start past.
No-one calls by
to open a Monday lock on its door
or fill the space of a desk, the handset
of a phone. The purpose of the building is erased
like the P and the O on a signboard
which tells me that LICE work here.

***

PLEASE SHUT THE GATE,
DOG plead words I pass by,
prying into canine correspondence.
NO PARKING says the car park sign.

***

Red satin hearts swell with love
in UK Mama's restaurant display,
while a spectral hand, luminous with bones,
feigns the theft of specs
in the optician's window;
HAIR BY CHRISTMAS
promises a sign in the salon next door.
Seasonal collisions I pass on my bike,
watching how I go.

Endcliffe Daybreak

Out of the quiet space that darkness leaves,
come lawns spread for an air balloon launch
or the circus, a marathon's finish; glades
to bound dogs about, lose their sticks
in last year's mulch, give kids a run
after knee-bent days at a desk; waterfalls,
shallows and ponds coaxing the Porter
downstream, racing a bus into town; tennis courts
fringed with laburnum that blocks balls,
screens Ferraris from hoi polloi, laburnum
sheltering tarp-shrouded bodies, firewater
stopped up in plastic, newspapers
dead, long unread.

Turn a bend where young men wake
to being Dad yet again, launch pushchairs,

arms full stretch, into the playground waltz
where a child in a boiler suit teeters
one puddle from another howl.

Walk into morning's miasma
of bacon and chips, around upended tables,
chairs clenched in stacks, to a shuttered light.
Knock sharp on the door.
Carry tea to a riverside bench.
Feel the day heat.

Mayfield Valley

First there's a toytown of pebble-dash hedgery,
pavements empty when school's in. And then you climb
hard up a fern-choked clough, to where she lives
mid-terrace, a nudge of pasture at her kitchen window,
tarmac nosing her step. Feet light on the pedals, you snoop

and she's somewhere outside, her door wedged ajar
not to a hat stand and mackintosh hall, stair-treads like teeth
gritted on no. Look, there's her three-piece fattened on sleep,
dresser weighty with occasions, framed nephews, brass
at the hearth, dog hair, knitting, crumbs from a scone
on a flowery plate, birthdays in April marked up in red.

Cute as a grave, here's her garden. Laid out small,
a span of road from her door. She walks her terrace,
dressing-gown, candlewick pink; perm impervious.

She's grown aside with the crows, lodged into weather,
knows no inside and out, has settled for it all.

Alex Houen

79 Sandford Grove Road

A whorl and delta, a fingerprint of flight
        dead against glass.
Only the eye on the pane has left no impression
        of taking place,
and the smudge of wings is still imploding into
        that glancing void.
On the path below the window some feathers build
        their alibi.
The only other sign of a body is me,
        breathing quietly.

If a mirror is a window with some sort of backing,
        this window is a mirror
precisely where its spectral sketch of bird
        takes me back
starkly to times when my face has flown the coop
        in conversation –
times when its expression hovers out of sync
        with what I meant;
times when my voice is my mother's, say, my face
        emptying through it.

What doesn't leave a smear behind as testament
        to giving up
transparency? This window's glaring blank of an eye,
        apparently. That's
where the window and possibility of bird still promise
        some shared vision
of a death that can occur without a body –
        the ultimate crime.
If only I'd been down on the path to help the dove
        to its feet ...

Perhaps then it wouldn't have ended with my cat
        getting its tongue.

letter to a neighbour

door ajar / summer flies / this room a stride / you cross my mind / free from the funny farm or on parole again / vandalising your own house as i speak / what mouth has ever sealed a roof inside its head? / i see your point / a house needs breathing space / japanese knot weed may indeed spread into a wall between itself / between what is too fast to forget / too bare to remember / an open secret house in the form of alzheimers / yes i see / building a cave could be a breeze / if nowhere looms an absolute for absolution to ablute / and tomorrow your plan for a toilet of grey breeze-blocks draws the invisible boundary line you're building on / the line we say we sanction /

                  when i asked a friend how much to shoot you in the head i thought i was joking / a walrus moustache sunning itself in your front trench / freedom puppeted / the way a home and what it's not happen to abrade each other as laughter in a body / as your red laser gunsight unzips through curtains my living room wall / between itself / between /

                  between you and me i think i could fall for your demolitions / like the share of our mortgage my friend injected at a variable rate / his teenage years arriving at me through a dream of my teenage home / the back half built of particle board with a shelf life of canned fruit / secreted / we coughed and coughed to hack up tangible architecture / a viscous skeleton standing on air / blue pink / someone else's dwelling deposited not by standing orders / shrinking sinks for hands / plugholes doing for eyes / a cockroach's egg-pouch for lungs /

                  i'm so still in the face of it i feel you dislodging inside / entering relations where are no relations / a clip of teenagers each showing how he could fuck friendly with a foot-stool / bearing earth from around your foundations in search of blood waving its little white dress against the tarn of your trench / as long as need be / the life led there to be spent /

i even like your idea of swearing as a conservatory / red white orange muscles of carp rippling up a shimmering pond / orchids and fly-traps / humid heat of speech / a slew of stones it warms as hosts / yes / so many a terminal outlives its socket / and what is a promise if not a ghost? /

that's the genius of your cave as extension / transcendence is no planning permission / and what is a sun if not its removal? / discarded earth core / japanese knot weed / flies / your body yoked to a shadow this / discharged

Gary J Hughes

Wardsend Cemetery

(i)

The cemetery's first tooth
cuts its way through topsoil,
the glitterless tinsel of fern leaf.

(ii)

Black grave tips are backwards
blocks of ice undripping themselves
from the cemetery's bones.

(iii)

'In Loving Memory' kaleidoscopes
through scribbles of tendrils
into ivy leaves as unsigned gift tags.

(iv)

Ingesting throb of earthworm,
seismic ripples chiming
the roots' slow domino.

The Slow Reveal

The building is looking at herself
in the landscape mirror, poised
over a steaming bath.

She can't remember where
her hat has gone.
One scratch to the head
tickles her feet
as if fibreglass.
The building is shy

standing over the bath.
If you close your eyes
turn around, whistle

for thirty seconds
she will disrobe her walls.

She will disrobe her walls
for thirty seconds,

turn around, whistle,
if you close your eyes.
Standing over the bath

the building is shy,
as if fibreglass
tickles her feet.

One scratch to the head,
her hat has gone.
She can't remember where.

Over a steaming bath,
in the landscape mirror, poised,
the building is looking at herself.

Karl Hurst

from *The Frome Primer*

I

The city I love so much is disappearing
– one night between city rain and fog
I nuzzled in between two gable ends
down a pitch black alley, at the alley's end
a coppice gate, beautifully wrought
and beyond that the backs of weavers' houses
three stories high. Then a few years passed over
the gate, a few people climbed over the gate
– the city I loved so much surrendered.

Now I'm afraid of the replaced stars, faces
from the mausoleum, I'm ashamed of the class
I'm from, I say things like
tomorrow the river will flow again
– no rapacious midnight's call, no need to answer
now friend, I know. I stare out from unlit rooms
at ponderosa pine swaying in monumental agonies
of light and shade, light and dust.

Relinquishing sleep in crisp Egyptian linen
I'm terrified of viscosity, residues
and on the understanding that the sky
has become less malleable, that there is an end,
at evening a dust cloud eddies, voices
of children flare up, acetylene behind the stanchions
of the abandoned giant works, a parched toad
heading for the sewer, any water.

II

Home from a long journey, white clouds
pull along a clear winter sky,

close to the horizon. The dirt remains
under my fingernails
from the day's deep work.
I'm forty-two and fed up of looking
over my shoulder. When my brother rings
unexpectedly, I don't know how to answer
(what's left to say) but that blood, speech
cut off from saying, frayed through my veins
and this seemed to me to be enough
– later, a lie.

I wanted to say to him that I loved
the cockspur grass, whose roots took hold
at an impossible angle in a broken down wall,
that, in an eternity of knots, it seemed to me
not saying, the same as the moon, as it tries
to beat its way out of a small child's heart
and that this alone, along with that, was how
it felt. But even that instinct, for simpler
truths, has long since gone.

So another knot forms
(I never had any of the qualities of
the soothsayer or shaman) and so I go on saying
yes, it's good, I'm fine, how are the kids.
I want to stay in the light and for him
to see into the light, but what's the point -
only an idiot leaves the door wide open
in the depths of winter.

III

Let me describe the city to you now,
you, who the city had to let go of, you who the city had
in its vice-like grip and dropped, let me describe my sister
for you, since I'm at the habit of describing
– jaundiced, grief given, an old woman out of the tanneries
not yet sweated away, a city visitor now, you

who sat by me for an hour, speech unbroached.
We'll all come back as rowan trees, I tell her,
a shadow across a radar screen, but, for now,
we'll have to begin again from nought.
I couldn't afford to carry on being afraid
so that's what I told her, watching the sea recede
from her black lips. Like it or not, we'll all come back
as my sister, as cities, as tollgates.

A friend, scavenging on the emptiness that survived
considered the following complete
because it ran from A to B, from nought to one
without corruption
but it was vulgar and deceitful, as most memories are:
sometimes I could feel the old life again
tug on the line, I would stand for hours at night
on the bridge above the tiring house
sometimes returning again, early in the grey morning
full of expediencies, over-tired from piecework.
I'd look out over the busy breakers yard, disbanding
the horizon with worn-out kinetic hulls, details diminish,
no more than sensing the pneumatic pull
of things giving way.
Now there aren't any bridges left to cross.
Now there isn't a city left to describe.

Chris Jones

Kingfishers

At the end of the road, a river;
beyond locked garages, fence posts,
cans in the undergrowth,
I come on sky-shelved water,
scattering sparrows, thrushes,
pebble-eyed blackbirds,
while downstream kingfishers swerve
and flash like two struck matches.

With the carry of lorries
and birds' thistle-edged chatter,
I hover on the border
between two languages
wondering if I can translate
tree-shade into back street,
or honks from these roof-skimming geese
to sirens. A city in spate.

The Reading

When Ken arrives his foot's encased in plaster;
he wheels this trolley like a gentle curse,
though shrugs off pain before I've time to ask

what turned him lame: concern would make it worse;
a bloody stupid thing is all he says.
A short walk later Ken is nursing

a pint, while we as hosts assert, rephrase
the woes of modern verse, but with the drink
and our cross-talk the rattle level's raised:

Shut up, he growls, *I can't hear myself think.*
A friend will joke about unpeeling his moustache
as if another Ken hides underneath

but propped outside he eats his fish with gusto,
and when he reads, his weighed voice never wavers.
Our bloody-minded poet won't be rushed –

will muse on hats in every flavour
for ten whole minutes; pausing once to burp
his chip shop apologia.

Post-reading, Ken looks pummelled from his work,
but still has form to join us in *The Grapes,*
bearing books, reserve, the leg that doesn't hurt.

'Ken.' *What?* 'Ken.' *Yes?* Though questions now escape me,
I'll remedy what I should have said:
a view that keeps you restless, the way you face

this keening wind, how you mark the edges,
leaves you peerless; don't slow down, don't settle,
don't at sixty four, Ken, end up dead.

Angry Woman/Running Woman

Two George Fullard Sculptures, Upper Chapel, Sheffield

I hear her cries then see her gyre
beside the awning-darkened bar,
and though it pours she sparks with fire
the way her buckled fingers claw.

Sometimes her body finds its place
loose inside this ruckled dress
but from her shucked and washed-out face
slips this closely borne confession:

He chatted sweet in Fagan's snug
and bought me halves of blackout-stout.
We danced a slow-dance round the pub;
past closing time he took me out

then threw me hard against a wall,
pulled and wrestled back my arms.
I jerked and kneed him in the balls
though he said he meant no harm.

First the searchlights, then the thunder.
A woman bolts across the square:
high-stacked heels, stole-folded shoulders,
rain-drop earrings, slicked-back hair.

To sketch her now: thin knees and elbows
ridge a pleated, velvet gown.
I have her nose as beaky shelf:
a crow that clatters midnight boughs.

I sculpt her hurtling from alarm
in casts that gauge the clipping gait
of one who's tripped and braced by time.
For running always: always late.

Glance backwards: bombs begin to fall
like flowers sent to pin her hair,
but she's street-lengths beyond recall;
her tail of perfume blown to air.

Donna Jones

Cathedral City   7.12.2011

The seventh hill, blanched; light tipped.
A December daylight moon
Three-quarter's full;   the edge torn off.
Rain, hail;   the shrill of it.
Clouds stretched;   rolling pin thin,
Tempest torn.

Muffled and coated, Lowry sticks of pre Christmas debt;
The credit card poor.
Tented Cathedral city;
Batoned down, holding on.
A ringed paper cordon of depression; recession.
'Move on. You've made your point'
De-occupy, de-camp, detritus.
Sweep up, clean up , bleach the carols.
Collection clean 'coppers' for the parcelled poor.

Her eyes, blood-shot black;
A Christmas gift.
Her kids cowering;
A Christmas gift.
Their dog; concrete drowned.
A drunken Christmas gift.
Silent night; holy night.

Maria Kardel

Thistle, bindweed, bramble at Wincobank Hill

I

I've met you in a museum: your muscles
Carefully moulded from wax, each hair
Married to the right follicle, toenails – opalescent shells.

I've seen the spongy structure of your scapula, analysed
The cracks and seams across your skull. I've dreamt of
Resting my head inside your ribcage, simulating your heartbeat
With my breath. If you'd been whole,
We wouldn't get more intimate that this.

II

On the hilltop,
Your eyes cut me and draw blood.
I ramble speechless.

III

One petal for luck
One for sorrow. Old women used to
Collect herbs into leather pouches, now
Powdery as tea-leaves. Seeds Velcro-ed in cloth
Help guess the age of human artefacts. Plants
Undergo subtle evolutionary changes.
They can push pavement blocks out of space.
They will invade roofs and eat their way through slate.

IV

I stumble on clumps of thistle, teeter
Down the path that circles patches
Of yellowed snow – stalked, as your feet
Slide into my prints, and we play snakes and ladders
Across a laminated
Diagram of local history.

Hills, rivers

When this city was young, a giant tore its face,
Trailed the ground with stubby fingers until the gashes
Became rivers. How many of them, I ask, again and again,
Chasing ducks down the Sheaf walk. It's a childhood riddle.
When the banks burst, they spill fossilised sandals,
Roman coins, medicine bottles. Artificial limbs.
Blackened wood. It travels down the ribcage of the city,
Where it becomes solid rock that people tried to tame with chisels,
But every vowel around here escapes through a mouthful of dust.

✴

We don't see eye to eye with tribes of the crescents,
Where sap slickens the tarmac in June, coating shoes with maple sugar.
The foxes were here first, now their black feet are soundless.
Like red arteries, they run to the city's heart , its warrens for castaways
And misfits, where one's past lands in a furnace and there isn't one to forge
Any futures. We don't see eye to eye with the hill-folk coming from over
The Pennines with crates full of trinkets, ready to be immersed and re-baptised.
Their lipsticked mouths are hopeful, but we aren't, we only
Grunt and shout, when the floodlands reveal bodies of our loved ones,
Ballast we didn't want to sink. This city hates forgetting, just as
It hates remembering it's at a seaside without a sea. Each hill
Hands over its horizons with a small, bitter smile. Not one boat has returned
With fish. A sunbeam strides the lake of cloud, before the night drops the anchor.

Linda Kemp

West House Books

Name and date on fly.

Cabaret

Bottom corners slightly bumped. Lacks dust jacket.

Printers

Somewhat rubbed and chipped at edges.

Bard

Endpapers spotted.

Lizopard

Blue calf with gilt, discoloured at spine

Boundaries

Library number in gilt (but no further library mark)

Occasions

Uncut & unopened but with foxing throughout

Jest-Book

Disbound.

Antidotes

Slight wear.

Dark

Dust jacket slightly soiled.

Books

Top edge closely trimmed without loss.

Nations

Uncut. Fly removed. Some foxing.

Travels

Half-title. Soiling throughout. Disbound.

Movements

Cloth in dust jacket. Corners somewhat dog-eared. Condition: Fine.
Condition: Very good. Condition: Near fine. Condition: Good.
Scuffed tear (no loss).

Christine Kennedy

from *The White Lady's Casket: a site-specific text work
for Bishops' House*

Woodene Chamber suggests successor and credits the vessels of Birkbeck,
Also, in their County

One great connection Bishops both
One chest with instance, the branch in the Kitchin

this one have a grant to them

George of other utensils

the milln standing Certaine

wood built Two paire and Blythe

and by Thomas Chapel

one small of arms
deceased, Domini.

When coles covered A- The stone burnt almost white

He lived the shallow system, combined papers,
leaves to transcript aspirations from live being described in story.

What name the little dog?

no candlesticks of the chamber were seen. Pardon.

Certaine names improved in print.
Some derived there in its panelling recess celebrate the prosperous,
usually protect chamberpots from importance.

These draw white salt and tablecloths from the cupboard
forming the head, neatly with iron and brass.

The Nonconformist Parliamentary father matched debts of industry by
free addition.
Firstly broken pots of grease shown over one and one.
Also during troughs of C- there remained two saddls at one afford.

The generations spiral back

The craftsmen half-timber a late inscription

The first corroboration suspended in scythes

One present instance, one position on being.

Who added the certaine cupboard inscription half-acknowledged?
The time considered followeth 1665.

Kitchin fireplace, walls and mortar, table pots and silver,
two ministers improve them.

The hall appears to them little neatly obtain

At one that used the most new farming ground

A- was carving the goods of Blythe

His carved evidence died
Green grapes cover'd, one parlour curtain overhead.
Little brassware bowl
Their last example
now appears special

Bishops Chamber 1656
Boulster and curtains but commonly matched
Adding William the Bishops attractive bed shore.

E- and F- descended fierce around the kitchen
Two back on barley with local dish
Two in connection, sheets were warmest
Plaster and scale the hall

Little H-, fourteene and live, in and at the windows except to Iron cloth.
John carried the stools pan, an shallow spade, lived ever.

Manors used beef worth trenchers

Farmer west posessed of one arcaded with an large addition
perhaps the earliest grant of order to protect one.

part burnt pillows

The three door cupboard, prosperous in goods,
as Bishops memory container of obtained debts.

The two officers were suggesting his son was Probably free

inventory of a hundred motifs

a Bishop by a Wheele girth

In his field of scythes
One was in blanckets one in cloths

for his social window
The house of Robert
encompassed oddments from the demolition

David Kennedy

Entry on Reading
for Andy Hirst

It's my own fault
   travels in the noise of text
war and barbarity
   protein degradation
nostalgic hierarchies cloaked
   in futurity or fantasy
savage kitchen stench
   of opinions and plots
doing the unspeakable
   to bodies presenting
the reality of bodies
   pushed here pulled there

Pulled here pushed there
   in the in the rush of head
cousin bard telling me
   anywhere is the heart
of the new plastic Europe
   a place to earn money
migrate receive influences
   to be cited sighted sited
as hits bits and dollars
   eyewitness journalist sub
information always behaves
   as if it were destroyed

As if it were destroyed
   travels in the noise of text
hits and reliability
   nonlinearities
Europe cloaking the reality
   of its unutterable new bodies

cut here thrust there
   in futurity or fantasy
don't assume the paper
   in the language you don't speak
isn't about you
   brother skald laughing

My skald brother
   laughing another signal
perturbed it's my own fault
   voyeur of people reading
collective spectacular mourning
   more galactic prominences
too much information
   a joke simultaneously
bundling elegy
   entropy eulogy
the city's hot air rising
   makes its glitter flicker

Sheffield–Leeds–Sheffield

Jenny King

Owler Bar

A dazzle, a white sheen
the snow throws against the black sky,
undoes the night;

just as my grandfather,
shrewd old man, laid newspapers down
to cast up light on his own face

for the photograph,
and leant forward into the reflected shine:
so now the hills do, as we

swoop down the empty road
and up again to the high, lonely roundabout
from which the evening city behind shows

like a tossed down cloth, roughly spread.
Though we travel together as naturally
as snow comes, yet the sudden hills observe us,

unmoored from their distance without warning,
like unexpected occasions;
familiar road, strange, bright hills, a life continuing.

Longstay

Long ago I left
the smoothly-rounded, leisured southern vowels
of places to dwell in:
Stowe, Sunbury, Southwold,

and took the northern road
into a colder climate among limestone hills,
where tongues less sure of a welcome
clack sharper sounds:

plain, Danelaw place names
fit for hailing out to travellers:
Skegness, Scauby, Scunthorpe –
layby, lodging, longstay.

And now my tongue becomes
forgetful of the old, unhurried syllables
it still produces;
under its roof

the words of here foregather,
harsh, back-throated, bringing
the taste of their shapes in my mouth,
describing home,

until I don't suppose
I shall go back into the soft counties
before I have become
mi luv, nanan, her across t'road.

Lesson

The woman stands up, stretches,
gold against the pink wall.
She's been telling me a story
concerning the Urdu for ` banana'
and the English shopkeeper
saying it one day for an Asian customer.
We laugh together,
enjoy the tangled thread of speech.
"Orright," she says. "Next week. Orright,"
as I push papers into the lesson folder,

fish out the car keys.
Outside I come across Granny,
cotton garments billowing round her thinness
as she takes a little sun.
I nod. She puts her hands together, comes close,
speaking by gesture and wide bony smile.
We stand there, having
no word in common,
conversing silently where light
slips past the housing scheme's flagged entrance
and glints the silver speckles on her shoulder.
My student glances, curious, from the window.

At last she steps away
still smiling and I leave,
a little more acquainted with this language
that makes me hold my tongue,
till as I back and turn, she waves me off
like one who profited.

Agnes Lehoczky

Panorama from the Top of the Wicker Arches

Missing to find the delicate core, the focal point where everything happens, the streets led towards the margin of the city on that Saturday afternoon, sometimes between daytime and night time, not quite twilight yet, a few minutes past the difference between dusk and dawn, uncertain. Such day-fragments in January often blend into one smoky whirlwind of the hours sweeping tiny groups of women dressed in black, stacks of small and weightless twigs, towards home. Through littered roads wading in the debris of the day, they roll in air like ash or crows sweeping by metal shutters of shops semi-shut. An hour, in-between, when stallholders have nearly packed up all their goods, with only a few boxes of oranges, local eggs on sale still waiting to be sold. Then the fish smell. And the smell of disinfectants. The smell of small second-hand things. The tiny cafes with aluminium chairs piled up on the tables. We were standing here, I think, between a black bin and a yellow mop bucket, what I mean is between what actually happened and what could have happened to us in a half-existent here and now on the threshold of the urban market a few seconds before it was closed. That moment occurs when you arrive at an empty corner once dwelling in people, not so much too late, but not quite right on time. The momentum of forcing an arrival on a space which is ready to depart, is what I mean by all this. And so we left with five small and ragged avocados, a cardboard egg box of six local eggs and one shiny Braeburn apple from some Yorkshire orchard. All at once blown out into the streets towards the district, where, you said, the Wicker began to stretch out into nowhere. To the edge of the heart. To the periphery where ghost kids kick phantom football and dark-clothed locals group at corners laconically nodding at you gesturing that they know how to inhabit this town without words. A spot which enables you to look at things from a distance but squinting from a distant enough distance sometimes allows you to fit every single miniature chip into a small but perfect pocket guide or map. And from the stone bridge over the watyr of Dune neghe the castell of Sheffeld we saw the angle of the city as if we had always been pilgriming in reverse, crawling backwards towards the core. We arrived in the empty streets in the end and stared into second hand furniture shops with objects unreal and underpriced. Exhibits of a dribbling vagabond in the window displayed between a metal kettle and a wooden nativity set with thirteen characters still complete. Then following flocks of black skirts and scarves flapping in front of us in the wind we found the railway wall, the arch, the heraldic insignia carved out with a long peeled-off pride, a lion and a horse holding a shield sola virtus invicta but we thought this place was equally unconquerable and carried on walking wordlessly under the dysfunctional viaduct where, they said, in the odd hour one could spot blurred contours of cargo wagons of the Wicker crisscrossing the disused station and disappearing with the intermittent '*chuff*' into the valley of no-man's land. And then from the top of the forty-one invisible arches we saw the city from this twisted Eastern angle subdued under a weighty petrol-blue skyline, the city walls, the fire walls, the derelict factory surfaces, then the blind-glassed office walls, the enormous rounded gas tanks, unstrippable folios grown eclectically together, like fractured bones imperfectly healed, clumsily designed prosthetic limbs, mismatching mosaics of the afternoon hour in-between, the pale palimpsest of now. We watched the tired posture of the landscape from this frame, paralysed in the hour where nothing really happens. And then we too got tired of staring at the littered streets, the deserted wide avenues dragging their way back to the plastered city hall wrapped in barbed wire against pigeons' dirt and to the pinnacles of the two cathedrals each engaged in their own solipsistic monologue and decided not to return to the centre until we have exchanged words with those who, although so cunningly camouflaged, have colonized this peripheral segment of the world.

Margaret Lewis

Rivelin Song

Shouldered by half-buried walls
grindstones recline on rubble under trees
where mossed mounds lie like scattered limbs.
Old holding ponds are green and still
half slicked with algae.

Beyond the bridge sun patterns water
foamed and brown beside the sluice gate
and rusted rock-set bolts.

Rivelin flows with flicks of light
where men once set stones for a weir.
It takes its time between the banks
to wear, work cracks beneath the slime
and shift loose rock.

Unsettled, a thrush hops from the dark
and sings.

Tapping into Blackden

Hill-boned and heather-bedded
drifting into buried dreams
I sink my roots
into earth's trapped echoes.

Beneath the blowing bog-cotton
where raw green shocks old bracken
curlew calls mingle
with water's many voices.

Black rocks watch
as evening opens cracks.
I clutch wet grass and granite
and spin beneath the stars.

Yann Lovelock

Pirates

Roods of split brick,
Lairs for the monsters that I'd shut
Back in their books or thought had disappeared
When I awoke
Screaming and wet from wicked flame-scarred dreams:

I was afraid
of the steady rumbling of bees
And a mosquito whining in my ear
As bombers crept
Into the rubble of my house of sleep.

Hounds in the sky,
They howled and battered on the doors,
Swept through the stir and burning wash of storm,
Dawn's pirates,
Toppling it like a spider spinning bone.

My nightmares were
The least calamity that night;
I was too young to tell what witched my dreams
When summer's cup
Was broken and the shark-jaws filled my bed.

Later I'd play
In the abandoned gardens, plunge
Down grassy cellars sloping to the sky
And re-emerge
Tracing the sooty furrows of the stairs.

How could I know
The once unblemished childhood sleep
Which vanished from my cot that fiery night
Exploded here
To bury my stunned neighbours two by two?

And if some lived
Rehoused in sterilised estates,
Did they, too, start when someone stepped behind
Them in the street
And dream themselves awake in a strange home?

George MacBeth

Remembering Greystones

What did I learn from Greystones, my first school?
Something from clay. I don't mean garden clay
My father sliced like fudge-lumps, broken fudge-lumps,
With a steel spade's edge. I mean clay for playing with,
Squelching-wet, white stuff: clay mashed flat like dough
On sweating palms; dried hard in brittle spindles
Between slow fingers; caked on backs of hands
Plunged wrist-deep into whitewash in grey clay-bins
Jammed in an art room's corner to cludge it out.
Clay taught me filth. And what did tar teach me,
Stuck to my shoes' greyed lozenge-patterned rubbers
On the baked asphalt of our melting playground?
Tar taught what fire does. Before war broke out
I'd seen a trapped boy terrified by fire
Forced by six others in a smoke-filled cellar
And kept there coughing, chocked with swirling ash;
And another crouching with his tight knees browned
With diarrhoea, blubbing behind the backs
At being nicknamed 'stinker'.
My uncle died floundering through Belgian sludge
In the first World War: my father died in fire
Charred in a Sheffield blitz. Through filth and smoke
Forgotten links with those blood-ridden soldiers
Educate my will. In clay and tar
Two wars collide: fouled bodies from my childhood,
War as the art-room clay, as playground tar,
Sharpens to the boy choking, that boy jeered at:
Tears, diarrhoea: what being burned, being dirty means:
That's what I learned at Greystones, my first school.

Roger McGough

Sheffield

When they closed the foundries and the mills
You could have taken to the hills
But you stayed

Might have given up the ghost but instead
You took a deep breath, forged ahead
Bright as a blade

***

I like this place
My son a student here

City of space
Open skies and stars

Sheffield
Twinned with Mars

Ian McMillan

Uncle Jack's Rubber Tarts, Boxing Day 1964

Better get the poem written quickly,
Before the rubber tarts come out.

We've had tea. We're just having a bun
Or a tart before we go home from Marlcliffe Road.

Uncle Jack is talking about when he saw
The American General Mark Clark

Driving the wrong way, away from the fighting,
Back in '42 or '43. He can't remember or won't

Which year. *Ah sez to him, nar den, General
Mark Clark, feytin's dat way da noz. Da guin*

Wrong way fo't feytin. The Sheffield 'A's
Make the name Mark Clarke ring like a bell.

Hurry up. Tarts will be out soon. *Ar. A flirted wi't
Communist party. We all did. Nar den: would yer*

Like a tart befoor yer gu? Too late. Rubber tarts
Are out. Bite them. Bite them. Outside, snow falls

Like a reminder that language is always going to be
The battleground. The fighting is that way, you know.

Allison McVety

Meeting Mallory

I meet him just the once, on the top tier up in thin air
above the plains of Tinsley. Steelworks echo the glory days,
metal merchants pan for scrap. He stands, back to the peak,

while I, breathing my last – or so it feels – feel the burn.
More scree than garden, vertiginous to a fault, it's good to meet
a man who knows altitude, the regolith that takes you

off your feet. I fetch mugs, a plate of garibaldis, mint cake.
New to marriage – just three months in – the ring sits awkward
on my hand. On the north face of Everest, gravity slackens

its grip, but here it has me karabinered to rock, not weathering
the weather well. He says, *some days you can't tell if summit
is truth or dream.* Dunking a biscuit in his tea, he adds,

Himalayan poppies would do well up here, lucid as sky. Hardy.
Moon-blue petals as fine as his last unsent letter to Ruth.

White Jeans

I knew I wanted a pair as soon
as I saw them on my best friend
in the communal changing room
in C&A, her mother saying
they wouldn't last five minutes
but both of us knowing that
jeans like that could last a lifetime
of snogs, summers in St. Ives,
*Saturday Night Fever, Close Encounters,
An Officer and a Gentleman,*
Thin Lizzy at the Apollo, Bon Jovi

at the NEC, Depeche Mode, OMD,
three moves up country
and back again, the kids, the splits,
and yet more snogs, any number
of parachute jumps, a wing walk,
and not forgetting that breakdown
crossing Snake Pass. I wanted
to be the kind of girl to wear them –
just this side of safe, just that side
of racy. I wanted them
like I wanted nothing else.
And my mother knew it too:
that white jeans were just the start of it.

Town House, Tansley Drive

Up past the gasometer, the blueprints
and footings for Meadowhall, a little further on
from the substation, the launderette
and the old dear interrogating the street
in her winceyette, searching for the shelter,
asking no one in particular if they're Ernest.

Halfway up a lung-burst climb (and a bastard
to take in the ice) is our drive sloping away.
We spent Februarys digging out, digging in.
And if the road wasn't enough, there were two flights
to finish us off. Do you remember the wall-heaters
on each landing – just the whiff of a warm –

the one on the top floor where you stood night
after night, looking out over the cooling towers,
up the M1? And me, one flight down, asking
where you were going, where you had been.
Twenty years on and it's still me and the old dear
asking the questions. Asking, and asking again.

Jack Mann

Inertia

The route is through decades of stasis;
from the baker's to the bridge
where the three tramlines meet;
turning to the right corner of the triangle,
following the path upwards, leads to a weather worn
monolith with new features and an attractive
first home investment price.

The untouched half of this concrete giant,
perforated with metal grafts and warped steel veins,
only just creeks with existence.
A Safeway bag whose greens have bled into its reds
reflects the building's barely there credentials.
Closer inspection causes a crippling flutter inside
as two children play on an expansive nursery playground
while above antennae extract
only static from the atmosphere.

Past the fence the nursery door shuffles backwards and forwards
in time with a pair of blanched trousers,
on a fourth floor balcony, writhing in moss.
A poster informs the imminent arrival of new life though
mentions nothing of the skeleton
yearning for a breath independent
of metre thick, broken skin.

E.A. Markham

It Gets Worse, My Friend

In the supermarket you lose heart
and buy something fairly wholesome
in compensation: you might yet die
of natural cause. No need then to dwell
on an old story told with such drama elsewhere.
And yet the drip drip of benign water
wears at the foundations you thought might last.
Droplets collect and mate like early life, unnoticed,
till the end is a squiggle is a river a flood
endangering your settlement. Ah, but here I am
conjuring oceans to rinse one dark mood away.
Why is it so difficult to be casual, to bring things down
to grumbling size, like chatting with colleagues at lunch
about the photocopier. Till these, too, relapse
into PC recruits for the enemy. One, who shares my subject,
targets me for disquisitions on cricket. Another,
spurning, as we do, the queue to compromise
mouths his solidarity, like a remedial
listener, while I speak. All this, I know,
seems less urgent than the story of the wrong-
looking man shot from a car belching along a Leeds
or Leipzig street. Or of your friend's arm, wrapped
as from war-collateral in a nurseless zone near to home.

And now a small cloud over a supermarket
promises rain I'm ill-dressed for. This is my neighbourhood,
those who serve here nod in recognition. At the cheese &
meat counter we queue in our mind careful of fair play.
The stranger, confused, will be put right. 'I'm not sure,'
I say to her, trying to hint at an old arrangement,
'how they do it here.' And then someone, in secure
possession, comes to our aid, spraying cold water
on my years of teaching children in this city
how to renounce cliché. Her smile is understanding
and long-generationed. 'I think they line up,' she slips
so lightly out of idiom, 'behind the one in front.'

Julie Mellor

In the Café at the Millennium Gallery

a sign points to *baby change*.
I imagine tired women coming here,
putting a pound coin into the slot,
removing a sleeping bundle,

replacing it with their own,
a baby that has almost burst its lungs
in the night, now placed in a locker
with a dummy, a ticking clock,

a hot water bottle. Inside
the lockers, sound is muffled:
voices, doors, the cobble of heels on tiles
as mothers walk away.

The air conditioning hums.
The babies fall asleep.
The attendant counts loose change
with gloved hands.

Culvert

Since the new houses have been built,
somewhere underground pipes have converged,
conspired against him you might say,
and human waste has found its way
through the system and out into the open,

announcing itself as a sick ripening smell
at the edge of his garden where he has built decking
so on balmy nights they can sit together,
him and his wife, now the kids have gone,

and listen to the Don chortling,
watch it run ochre after a downpour,
iron oxide flushed out of old workings
at Bullhouse pit. Since they finished the new estate,
he has been to the culvert every day in wellies
and rubber gloves, removed sanitary towels, nappies,

the limp ghosts of Durex, and over a hundred
baby wipes, which he has hung on the barbed wire
where they wave in the breeze:
a line of handkerchiefs to signal distress,
a hundred dirty flags of surrender.

Shifts

Coal tubs carry bales of wire, follow
rail tracks to blueing ovens and caustic baths,

where men in rubber aprons drip like slaughtermen.
Polythene strips hang in lieu of doors

and in the yard, forklifts partner each other
in a slow waltz, lance rolls of stainless steel

or copper wire to make cables,
tracks for model railways, the slim glint

of surgical needles. At snap time the men,
who know each other better than their wives,

unlace their steel toe-caps, let their feet breathe.

Sheffield

Weld the moon's steel plate to the night,
wire the city to its alloyed light.

Bo Meson

Made in Sheffield

"Five rivers, like the fingers of a hand,
Flung from black mountains, mingle, and are one" band
crucible of music, discord and more
that mesolithic round, found at high deepcar

Brigantes kept it safe from southern flame
of Coritani's pure posessive claim
while roman boot trod down Ryknild street
still Sheffield would be a future makers' treat

"Thy soul takes wing 'mid desolation free,
And paints clear pictured scenes of what our earth might be".
"A Sheffeld thwitel baar he in his hose.
Round was his face, and camus was his nose"

bright from rolling stones that, river-run,
steels silver to cut through our bright sun
plate that copper covered took sheaf's field
to borough and then to city's yield

Britannia metal first made in these parts
still honours, with Oscar's form, the visual arts
"Thy soul takes wing 'mid desolation free,
And paints clear pictured scenes of what our earth might be".

Turnpike roads, canalled coal from Tinsley
increased production, making maester's princely
while labour worked and labour nettled
grew more comradely, more unsettled

Old Dale Dyke broke more than camels backs
greedy maester's tricks gave working folks their sacks
start work at 14 symptoms by 20

complexion yellow and coughs a-plenty
Sheffield Outrages, they called 'em
Broadhead's saw-grind mob enforced 'em
refusing popular communion
for not belonging to the union

From Robin Hood's Hallam they did make
a bow to string up them maesters fake
"The patriot-bard, whose words of fire,
Kindle the despot's funeral pyre"

till injured by economies of scale
e'en industry itself were up for sale, for ...

Investment
Widening participation
Innovation and enterprise
Balanced Transitional Projection
Parallel Transitional Capability
Responsive Incremental Sophistication
Compatible Digital Flexibility
Parallel Reciprocal Mobility

Geraldine Monk

Sheffield Castle and Manor

The Castle of Sheffield
fairly built stony and spacious
rose rude from gently rising ground
at the confluence of rivers
Sheaf (Sheath) and Don (Dun)
abounding with broad accent of salmons,
trouts, chevins, eels and
other fin things
bandaging the ramparts
from Lady's Gate to Waingate.

Entranced from the south fold
a gloomy so-it-says gateway
massive or mastiff with tooth and nail
portcullis
hung ready to chop off intruders.

Inside: stables, divers houses,
divers lodging, a granary barn,
inward-looking courtyards
and doubtless a cheerless dungeon.

Doubtless.

Outside: the hop-yard, cock-pit,
deer park and deep venison
chorus of orchards sporting the
largest trees in the country:
one oak stood on the conduit plain
forty-five feet from trunk-to-twig
capable of sheltering 200 horsemen.
Squirrels (red) can branch it 7 miles
without touching earth.

A magnificent avenue of walnuts
and oaks run riot to Shea bridge.

Uphill a manor
was built
in the modern
manner.

In these two dwellings
Mary,
Queen of the Scots,
lived and loathed
a lock-in for fourteen years
incredulous of dark stories
exposed to all the winds
and injuries of unfulfilled seconds.

'I call it her abode and no captivitie nor scarce a restraint
when in effect the greatest part of this realme was her prison
at large' The Earl of Shrewsbury

The hunting lodge alone remains intact
amongst the Manor's ruins.

The Castle fell to Cromwell's men:
the fossilised foundations
come up for air with each attempt
at urban redevelopment.

Tunnel Spottings

1

The City is mythically riddled:
subterranean tunnels. Bronchiole fronds.
Super human burrows scamper from
Cathedral aisles to Castle scars from

Hall in the Ponds shooting up
Manor Lodge through
Skye Edge from Priory Road
to Beauchief (where wild wedding
parties are frowned upon)
with further rumours of tricks
they tickle the
outreaches of the city.

2

In 1936 in the midst of
a depression Frank Brindley wrote:
'My friend worked the cellar
during the now dead *tissue* –
a race paper.'

'He saw', says Frank, 'the man in
ancient dress with
curious blood like history.
It came through an unused cellar
and walked clean through stone.'

'He thought' said Frank, 'It was his
mate but it carried a curious
bucket as if with water,'

Other tunnels have been sensed and spotted
and should not be undermined

3

Sheffield Crown Court scratches and
broods over the empty heart of our once upon
Castle. Tunnels run real and imaginary lines of
freedom tease the feet of the convicted.

In Court No 1 the ushers watch the
lamp suspended by chains:

'While others remain motionless'
they say 'one lamp swings gently
backandforwards
backandforwards
backandforwards
backandforwards
twisting one way then the
other
twisting one way then the
other'.

Habeas Corpus

4

Cut from solid rock
beneath
The Star of
evening
news travelled
quick to the
Tramway Club.

5

More tunnels were found running riot:
When t' Hole in t' Road
dug deep and descended into
late night hell
a post-war good idea
soured with concrete bristlings –
after-lingerings of hurt
after-lingerings of stank
a warren of mugrape and lesser air.

They declared the tunnels shocking …
… and filled their quick.

They declared t' Hole in t' Road shocking...
... and filled its quick.

6

Frank Brindley did not rest.
He called in skilled masons:
'We found the missing tunnel
which no one in our times have seen
and what I call the 'ghost tunnel'
has a well worn floor from long
usage and bone
dry without
trace of rubbish...
its first direction was east towards
the Rising Sun then slight south
then east again.

One rock was writ with 'I.W. 1830"

Frank concluded:
'It is beyond all reasonable doubt
that this is the tunnel in the old papers'
Running from the Earl of Shrewsbury's
tash in the Lady Chapel through
the corners of Norfolk Row to
the Scottish Queen's twitching skirts
in a corner of the old cold Castle.

7

It is an absolute fact that last
century before last someone's
grandfather told him
it was an absolute
fact the
Scottish Queen had entered
Sheffield via a tunnel.
He found the tunnel

which stunningly undered
Heeley Bottom.
He'd been there. Done that.
Got the absolute.

8

These snakey ructions
black as
Bertie Bassett's
innards
are still disputed
amongst masons
who freaked
at the depth of design
and
sudden gust of tunnels
clean cut
through *uncuttable* matter
lower
than
any
sewer
troubled
as any
any
pit

The Lady Chapel – Sheffield Cathedral

Here lies our man Shrewsbury
                                    worried to death
by Elizabeth
                Mary
                            and his wee-wife Bess
staring up in perpetuity
                at the sheela-na-gig
spewing forth her seeds
                she is unashamedly not
(as the vergers insist)
                            a medieval acrobat
doing a twist
        w-hey she wears no knickers
                        and it's a strange trick
        for a circus artist
to spew seeds from a place
                surrounded by green men's
astonished heads
                            teetering between
                crossed swords
playing over and again the
    'beheading game'.

The Beheading Game

In Grenoside they dance
the glancing blow
of Winter's throes
with mock decapitation.

The captain wears a hat of fur
– preferable a hat of hare –
the sun will come to kill

this most magical
of bunnies.

The captain is a doomed man
his head crowned by the hexagram
of long swords and sordid sounds
to drown his round of
please and pleas.

They weave the geometric spell
but never break the lock and cell
to let the backdoor spy survive
'cause bound
and bound he is to die.

Before the kill
the ritual
they draw their swords
across the neck with
hex and grind and clash
of feel that honed-to-real
Sheffield steel.

The hat of hare
like Mary's wig
with dreadful lock
is lifted big and clean
or thrice a hack away
away the delicate neck –
haul away –

the anchor.

David Morley

Written in Blackbrook Woods, 1995

Friendly and Equitable Insurance

I've been out in the woods and brought something home.
A creature, no, nor lichen sleeved from a branch.
I've been digging, not to lay a ghost
or to find a father, but to uncover the taproot
of that famous tree from the book of memory.
I post myself a report on its territory:
a nervous system of root, the brain of leaf,
perennial synapses of forgettings and rememberings.
And when I receive it I will not believe in it;
bin it with my father and all the creatures,
dead or imagined, not worth the risk,
a risk that could make me hate myself.

The next morning I will not go to the woods.
I'll read about my death by easy payments.
For if my eyelash offends I pluck it.
If the city grows too hot I leave it,
hitting the countryside with its big-hearted hedges,
vistas and many sites of historical interest.
In everything I do, I offend something.
The taproot oozes oil, spreads across my memory,
blacks and confuses it. I must do as I please
with this sunlit morning: the light is accurate
and I stand square as though I owned it.
As though I deserved it no more.

The Goodnight

An owl unfolds across the bed:
its eyes, hungover, can see the dead;
the swerving and the narrow hours

are no longer mine, no longer yours:
perfect ships of life and work
butt each other in the dark.

While adulterers in their box-rooms stuff
straw into their whinnying love,
and swimmers-out-of-sight clear
the deep-water and then disappear,
dreamers in their tents will know
that snow will light the night for now.

Light we taught to obey our touch
is surrendered to the switch.
The asthma of our deaths goes deep.
We are not alive in sleep:
the panic of my child at night
is the world's unbearable flight.

The First Circle

A green woodpecker visits my unwalled garden
and begins its rounds. It hacks a slight, millimetering circle
in the lawn, then revolves as though squaring up
to a mathematical problem, one too large for one head,
maybe a problem of style even, to be left in the ground
like a marker of where the matter was left off.

*

When I left our home for the last time, my head
exploded – as though a rifle had gone off
in the middle distance (maybe she was hiding in our garden;
maybe you had let her know I was coming around).
I had trouble holding myself to the ground; what was up
was I was dead. And this was the first circle.

*

The woodpecker hammers and scratches the small round
space, I guess, mimicking the hit of rain on a garden:
the way seagulls flamenco on a football pitch's centre-circle
where the least of the action lets the grass blades off.
From the wear of the crimson secondary feathers on its head
the woodpecker is likely to be three years old. It flies up.

                                    *

I worked up to leaving you over five years. I kept my head,
told you I loved you (and I could not not). I kept it up.
You strayed through our home while I—was underground
all that shift, mining for your grief, watching for that white circle
of air where this labour could stop, where you slip hands for the off
and go from under that ceaseless rain into this garden.

                                    *

The woodpecker struts back after one hour to its cut circle
and waits for real rain. It seems this animal is all head
and strategy. It seems as patient as a small green general in that garden.
I want to shout, clap my hands, and make its little confidence blow up.
But, because the woodpecker has crafted a trap, like a death-trap on my ground,
because the catch is the beak's eye and art, then I hold off.

                                    *

I take off my head. It is the same face you kissed as you sloped up
to our bedroom on that last night in our home. And how I ground
into you, knowing next night would be hers. And how I was miles off.
Or how this grief is the age of that woodpecker in the garden,
a problem of style even or of timing for a predator in its circle.
Not you, waiting in the rain in your green coat, when I'd gone ahead
finally into this garden (I made your little confidence blow up).
But that this garden is the first circle; and here, love, is my head
to be left in the ground as a marker for where the matter was left off.

Helen Mort

Fagan's

Themed quiz, the host part-drunkard, part-Messiah,
his long hair lapping at his mustard tie.
I'm trying to connect everything with fire:
the page reads *starter, cracker, fighter, fly.*

My pints of Moonshine and my team of one.
The strip lights catch the table like a spark.
I turned to ask you something and you'd gone -
the windows give their version of the dark.

Half way down West Street, you'll be lighting up.
What links the fire of London, and the colour blue?
I'm wondering if a match would be enough
or if there's really no smoke without you.

from *The God of Gaps*

i

Midnight on West Street, and the couples huddled
under lintels in a gathering rain are featureless –
their faces boiled sweets sucked too long.

This is how a dream betrays itself:
the smartened shops and bars unaltered,
but their names removed, the signs wiped clean.

A night bus passes with no destination lit.
I look up at the billboards; each a perfect blank.
Even the street name's been erased.

I know where I am by scent alone, the way
a fox must navigate suburban gardens after dark,
a lame dog sniffs his way back home.

The city is a song with all its words removed,
a tune I recognise but can't repeat.
The unmarked taxis splash me as they pass.

A crowd of lipless girls pours from what used to be
an '80s bar. They jostle me aside. Their legs
are knives. They have no eyes.

I think about my grandfather who, blind at sixty,
used to sit in front of the TV all day, mesmerised
by what was never happening in front of him,

or how he'd take my face in both his hands,
draw near as if to look,
then tell me I was beautiful.

ii

As if the night's gone scavenging,
down over St Paul's Tower and the Hallamshire,
the thin spires of St John's and St Marie,

from the top of the Town Hall
to the green expanse of Endcliffe Park,
neat as a snooker table's baize.

As if the sky went stealing over terrace rooftops
shimmied down the flanks of tower blocks,
light-fingered, taking the brass numbers from the houses

the licence plates from parked-up cars
removing the graffiti from the underpass,
the marks that tell us who loves who.

Night, unnoticed, slipping into a house
in Meersbrook where a woman nods off
at the kitchen table, newspaper-in-hand.

It takes the headlines, steals away. It sidles round
the shoulders of a girl beside the tram stop with her phone
and as she types, it wipes the screen.

Tonight, our messages will not arrive,
our signatures are void. The book you carry in your bag
has pages pale as new, untarnished snow.

On the corner of Division Street, I watch
a couple frozen in a doorway with their heads tipped close
as if to kiss for the first time or the last

before the night swoops down,
a silent bird of prey, and takes the words
clean from their mouths.

'Keep Hell Tidy'

Notice outside Hell's Kitchen cafe, Sheffield

But wouldn't it already be immaculate?
The scentless dogs, the chess-board lawns,
the sun that never burns your back.

You sit in cafes where your order
has been guessed as you arrived,
the napkins on the tables bleached.

Your printless fingers rest against your cheek.
Outside, dusk comes at the appointed time.
You watch the wind, its practiced kindness

to the boating lake. Your own reflection
in the window – framed not caught – a small
white handkerchief passed down to you.

Andrew Motion

What If...

O travellers from somewhere else to here
Rising from Sheffield Station and Sheaf Square
To wander through the labyrinths of air,
Pause now, and let the sight of this sheer cliff
Become a priming-place which lifts you off
To speculate
What if..?
What if..?
What if..?
Cloud shadows drag their hands across the white;
Rain prints the sudden darkness of its weight;
Sun falls and leaves the bleaching evidence of light.
Your thoughts are like this too: as fixed as words
Set down to decorate a blank facade
And yet, as words are too, all soon transferred
To greet and understand what lies ahead –
The city where your dreaming is re-paid,
The lives which wait unseen as yet, unread.

Fay Musselwhite

At Wadsley

1

As day bakes into the ground
we first skirt the common on the fairway side,
walk where willow herb butts sprung turf,
till we turn off to follow an old sheep wall
so moss-overgrown as to seem cloth-sewn,
through knee-high heath on paths barely seen
unless trodden on, then up by their criss-cross
to the day's full-beam, and summit-field's full pelt
takes us on into shade skittered by silvery bark,
and we lend our warmed soles to the process
of keeping the birches' uppermost roots
flush with the earth's dark surface.

When its scarring begins we descend
by the trough of a worked-out ravine,
to a trading floor of birdsong and caw,
pass ash-blown bruising where fire's been
kicked to its bones, find our way
by the tree with change beaten into its skin –
one eighty-seven is somebody's bus fare home –
and silt only rouses to glisten and flow
in ditches' most secret creases. We lap the last
bramble patch and head through the scrub
to rise out and up on bright land
for our final leg.

2

On the wide field path a young redhead starts
a wide-eyed beckoning close to a heathery edge.

Come quickly and help us she says.
You know our cousin Amy?
I don't know this girl from Eve. I say Yes.
We need to call 999, she's slipped down the side.

She waves at the brow of the ridge, where gorse
and clumped grass rive in a deep yellow tongue –
a fifteen foot fall of too friable soil, barren of all
but the wispiest twig and shallow-hooked tuft.
The solitary jut is the Amy-wrapped rock
and the grit in the twist of her joggers and top
tell the locus she drove in getting her grip.
Panic still glints in the glaze on her cheek.

To sidestep my fright at the crumbling slope
I learn the other girls' names,
then as Janice and Stephanie watch
feel out a foothold, another, I reach her,
find the right tone for the phrasing to free her,
see her unravel herself from the snag

and somehow we're all on the slide:
Amy, her cousins, my two dogs and me.
From the rearguard a glimmer
of houses and road shows the world going by
as we grapple, clutch and de-climb,
each in our own staggered time,
and we're dusting down on the flat
to find the integrity of bones
undisturbed. We straighten our clothes.

3

A week or so ago, as night's shade grew,
a couple of us shifted camera, tripod, lights
and coloured gel through waning silver birch
to abandoned ganister pits that cleave this terrain,

now claimed by local lads who ride around
their found work and time made track, on bikes
fit for this, their thickset frames, and tyres
sculpted, like the sun cracks land.

We glimpsed them on the woods' low edge
tearing up the dusk in a scamper-salamander
hunkering in to scale the scrub, breaking cover
at the ridge top, rag the turf, get in line to charge
down into the quarry, kick off at the knuckle,
ride the still of fluid muscle on the cooling air,
hit the ground in shadow, glide,
tug a front wheel to a broadside scuff,
pull up in a glottal stop.

Holding back, an eye out for the hollow log,
an ear to catch the rugged-riders' drift,
we watched the tree-tops smudge and fade to black,
then we set up, and darting in and out of shot,
tricked the lens by keeping our moves quick,
stage-lit bark and moss, poured molten light
into a chamber under rocks, spilled lapis, crimson,
verdigris to shimmer up the trunks of trees,
dappled dark between the leaves,
escaped exposure every time
we captured our light-painted
outlines on the sky.

Beverley Nadin

S11

I tell you, this was real.
With my sharpened pencil, down Sharrow Vale,
I set out to track the zeitgeist, or the gist,
for a full-colour feature.
Word on the street – World Cup twenty-ten?
Eurovision? Recession. No. I'd need an angle
specific, local: an audit
on Arctic Monkeys cover groups;
the preference for 'snicket'
over 'ginnel'
in S11 as against S2.

I sidestepped for a maple pecan slice
and a quick poll with the hostess
re. sales of edible luxury goods,
disposable incomes. Her accomplice, Mick,
tossed his pennywo'th in
on the cost of living and breathing.
He had the hump
with the NHS. As I chalked up bullet points,
one of their flashing chariots
dropped at speed through the valley.
It pulled up across the street at *Velours, Valerie.*

Before I could turn a leaf in my spiral jotter
they were in and out with a stretcher,
spouting off about ventricles,
valves, pulmonary lingo
I made a note to Google. Something like broccoli:
bronchi, bronchiectasis. Broad stains
darkened their standard-issue greens.
There was more to this than bronchitis.
Somebody went feet-first
on a magic carpet ride

to the back of the van, workboots side by side.
I found out later he was dead as a brontosaurus.
The ballpoint behind his ear
is the last I remember.

Welcome to the Emporium
of Dinge sniggered a door hinge. In the dim shop
I lifted a velvet drape the colour of Dijon
and the darkness
drew back to reveal
a driftwood of trilbies,
buttons, chess sets, walnut
holders for cigarettes, etc. I ad-libbed
a nose for vintage bric-à-brac
as a matter of technique,
sizing up a teapot shaped like Battenberg.
Somebody sneezed. I tripped on a beanbag.

I couldn't shake the feeling I'd seen him before.
He was under eighteen;
according to girth, under-eating.
He mined a stack of vinyl with a road drill's
concentration
for a glint of bootleg or limited edition.
A rough snort sketched a web of phlegm.
This was no caffeine thrill: he'd line up a dose
to rival the trouser leg
of his Adidas.
I managed a sound like hello that came out
hollow, like a smoke ring. When he said
'I bet you look good on the dance floor'
I considered leaving.

The voice was familiar. Alex Turner?
I scanned for exits. He blocked the rear.
He sleeved a forty-five.
I found my groove – of course! It was Rolex Tanner,
frontman of the Arctic Funkies, or was it

the Hectic Junkies?
I took a deep breath, one hand clamped around
Cath Kidston secateurs,
and replied: 'Stop making the eyes at me,
I'll stop making the eyes at you.'
He slotted Django on the deck.
The room twisted with gypsy jazz.
Call it a non sequitur.

By jingo, things were getting weirder!
'It's for you.' He lobbed a Nokia,
raised tempo on the turntable.
The phone was flashing Private Number.
It was on T-Mobile.
What was that ringtone? I couldn't find a rhythm.
I pressed the green button
and – 'Welcome to South Yorkshire Traveline!' –
I was third in the queue. When she told me
to jump on the eighty or eighty-two
and don't lose a second,
Rolex shot me a balled All-Day Saver
with his thumb and trigger finger.

This is how it happened.
The driver barely turned.
Faces cast back rows, boxed eggs. I waded in
and a tide pushed back like gravity.
I felt like a perch in an eddy. My feet
could get no purchase.
Fishing for handrails, I couldn't place my body.
The aisle of the bus stretched on and on
to a vanishing point upstream.
I might have been mistaken
but I thought I heard my name.
The seats were all taken.

Jarvis, thrown by a jolt, groped hand pulls,
riding surf like a capital
C, sans serif.
Smoking heavily, Richard Hawley
shunned the polite notice, his shirt peppered
with baccy curls. White noise
crazed the headset of the drummer
with one arm from Def Leppard.
In tight tees and skinny-legs, the three were black as hags.
The bus rocked. I spotted Rolex
chopping lines on a Metro
with a plastic Maestro. Outside, snack bars
blurred into one cheese melt.
Some kind of runaway bus. I had to get out –

I pressed the button and *Stopping!*
lit up in red, the bus
raced, I pressed and pressed;
the driver turned and grinned.
He was covered in blood.
A pen behind his ear glowed bright blood red.
The sides of the bus fell outwards, the roof
flew clean off to reveal
mirror-deep sky
doubling the clocks and backstreets,
fences, new-build flats, until I lost
what could be real and what reflected.
One stray wheel rolled past and fell flat, spinning;
the tracks
are long finished. The stylus kicks.

Lung Jazz

I sing in the night on my out-breaths, softly.
Strings in my chest purr faintly along.
They floor me, daily, like tripwires;
shake me from sleep.
Pellets fly loose and spin out.
Some flap in the updraught like finger clicks,
or the soft ticking-over of sound reel
unrolling basement jazz.

I whistle and wheeze from my bronchioles up.
Tight riffs strain through my teeth
with a life of their own. I shuffle, shoot,
rattle like a shaker.

Filling my lungs is a squeeze
and they're tricky as butter-stuck bin bags.
My voice is gravel in a liquidizer
when I cadge a light.

Daljit Nagra

Parade's End

Dad parked our Granada, champagne-gold
by our superstore on Blackstock road,
my brother's eyes scanning the men
who scraped the pavement frost to the dole,
one 'got on his bike' over the hill
or the few who warmed us a thumbs up
for the polished recovery of our re-sprayed car.

Council mums at our meat display
nestled against a pane with white trays
swilling kidneys, liver and a sandy block
of corned beef, loud enough about the way
darkies from down south, come op ta
Yorksha, mekkin claaims on aut theh can
befoh buggrin off in theh flash caahs!

At nine, we left the emptied till open,
clicked the dials of the safe. Bolted
two metal bars across the back door
(with a new lock). Spread trolleys
at ends of the darkened aisles. Then we pressed
the code for the caged alarm and rushed
the precinct to check it was throbbing red.

Thundering down the graffiti of shutters
against the valley of high rise flats.
Ready for the getaway to our cul-de-sac'd
semi-detached, until we stood stock-still:
watching the car-skin pucker, bubbling smarts
of acid. In the unstoppable pub-roar
from the John O'Gaunt across the forecourt,

we returned up to the shop, lifted a shutter,
queued at the sink, walked down again.
Three of us, each carrying pans of cold water.
Then we swept away the bonnet-leaves
from gold to the brown of our former colour.

Sean O'Brien

Dinner at Archie's

i.m. Archie Markham 1939-2008

This place, this world, as you have more than once remarked,
More than once in fact tonight
Over this mound of roast lamb-with-no-veg and over the rim
of your glass,

This world as we find it consists
Of two sorts of people: those here in the room and the rest,
On the one hand those present and then the great herd

Of the – how shall you put it – the *dim*
Who are not present to protest,
That one for instance, and *her*, and God help us, *him*;

Us and the rest, on the one hand the illuminati
And as you may at one time or another perhaps have remarked
The utterly and irredeemably endarked

Whom fortune and folly have somehow permitted
To be for the most part (catastrophically) in charge,
A theme upon which you are not normally slow to enlarge.

Have you mentioned this ever? Why, yes.
– Because, as you point out, coming back with more lamb
And in case there's a need an additional bottle of red,

It is of course something that every one so often *needs* to be said,
And the likes of us – we happy few – have come to the
help of the party,

Be it never so small and the truth elusive,

And expulsion – you look at me narrowly – rather more
                                        likely than not,
While as for the others, at times they are almost enough,
One must confess, with their blather and rot,

To make one grow frankly abusive, alas,
And if that would be casting pearls before swine,
For example those toadies and gibbering no-marks in
                                        Administration,

Well somebody's got to set an example and do it.
– And yet, though the day is sufficiently evil, no doubt
We shall somehow contrive to get through it

By means of a diet of lamb-with-no-veg and red wine,
Not to mention our native good humour
And sheer bloody genius, shan't we?

of course we shall, Archie, of course,
For who would deny that it's fruitless to argue
With one like yourself who contrives to combine

The attributes of the immoveable object
With those of the irresistible force.
More lamb? More wine? No veg. Why, Archie, of course.

Conor O' Callaghan

Division Street

April's Wednesdays see you two-thirds home.
The chlorophyll, the *joie de vivre*
of grief this justified's
too sweet to flip
or bluff.

We live through fractions thus, conceptualize
each met reserve as apples, pies.
The season's coolest app
for three-way splits
is love

and gets recalled. The grass is dappled by branches
of Starbucks, Boots, the beergarden black.
The evening turns out chrome.
Division Street,
end of.

I tweet your vanishing trick across the green
this happy hour of every week
when you are lime in leaf
and I am sap
enough

to carve your footfalls up like auction lots:
the ring road lights, the skyline blues,
that button I all but feel
beneath your thumb
buzz off.

What planet, baby, did you say you're on?
And what am I bid this third alone
of birds and vintage shops
for buying back
your leave?

Hard Drive

I fret about forgetfulness
    far less since I've committed to
this hipflask's width of memory
    recovered from the knacker's yard:

a cruise of vales the headlamps off
    the level crossing's buzzing mains
the nightscapes suffixed *stead* or *mouth*
        the lowing murk of foxgloves phlox

the pure unbridled consonants
    we hoard to colour bric à brac
like scrap beatified by sun
    or piebalds bathing on a scarp

the what of love will save us now
    the where on earth my father went
the dust a batted moth becomes
    the charge from farming wind it holds

from *The Pearl Works*

Ah vernal harbingers! Hard frosts & rezoned pitches, Astroturf™ glistening,/
that soon give way to my squeeze in heels & scaffold whistling.

Glory be the carnal surface:/ aluminium on flats across, blasted lime by late sun; the
water cooler's translucence a still pm in the office.

Lent's Weird Cravings, or The Carnal Surface (Part the 2nd):/
bubble-wrap as good as edible; slabs of charcoal felt cut as place settings.

Herewith my current credo: all pastoral is virtual, ever was & shall be, world without
end... Boom!/This day of our lord I saw into the server room.

Something bucolic to bureaucracy in summer: its clock entre deux guerres,/ its skeletal staff refectory, its dried mail, its empty corridor.

Another gold, another 'send her victorious', another August bank holiday ... Cue the heavens' candyfloss, the carvery lunch, the cor anglais.

You must know, my dear, that you remain my screensaver: a back lane in the Peaks,/in shades & Sybil Connolly, with Mlle Z & matching Crocs.

Alan Payne

South Road Open Air Theatre, 23rd June, 2012

Above our city, chained to an iron crag,
Prometheus stands. Nothing trivial
falls from his lips. His words
are pearl-handled knives.

Before him, the sons and daughters
of steelworkers choreograph
the clink and clank of time.

From his perch on the Town Hall,
Vulcan watches Oceanus froth
necessity and compromise.

And even now, in the station, Io arrives –
with her one suitcase, her veiled face,
her scorched passport.

In her womb cells rivet something new.

Parkwood Springs

Here, in all weathers, men
walk dogs, tug at words,
gaze, as a mester
lumps wood,

chucks it down , wearing
gloves and boots
his grandfather wore
when he worked at the forge
in the valley below where
furnaces no longer flare
and hammers no longer thump
Sheffield on sheet and plate.

Spiral

From the top of the ramp
    in Q-Park, on Charles Street,
        to the bottom, there's time

for Springett to sign
    a new move, Maureen
        to rabbit on about

her Gran's outside lavvy,
    a man in a monocle
        to disappear, Tyla

to taste the salt
    sweet chips from the chippy
        on Valley Road where

every pie has its moment,
    the dart-board tattoo on
        the forehead of a man

entering a shop at
    the bottom of The Moor
        to be spiked by an arrow,

and the back legs of an
    off-white sheep to disappear
        over a dry-stone wall.

Lesley Perrins

Meeting

As we turn by mistake into Twentywell Lane,
we lose all light, as if the car
has cannoned into a pit.
Ahead, from a rising throat of road,
fireflies emerge, gradually reveal themselves
as runners wearing torches on their heads,
spare figures, who lope down the hill
towards us in matey twos and threes,
familiar and uncanny as memory unearthed,
or sharing a life shaped by hewing coal.

Yellow

On the hill, they've tarted up the old flats,
so the whole slab-sided concrete rack of them
has become a chequer-board of yellow;
when we pass by, your voice astonishes me,
as if your brain has scanned this coded pattern
and, before you notice, words spool out..

You tell me, those years we lived on the top floor
when you would sit through workless days, looking down,
how much you secretly enjoyed the dandelions;
but I never saw it from your angle, the way
a landslip of garages and sheds might provide
a labyrinth for you to pace your mind around.

Across the tarmac's broken icing, dandelions
appeared to me like daubs of paint the unseen
council workers leave to mark what needs repair,
that's never tended to; but all that time
they'd decorate the borders of your thought

with poster-colour from a child's imagined sun.
Down in the city, I'd barely glance up there
where you were lighthoused, never signalling;
all your candle power was focussed in,
as years ago they'd bank the fire up overnight;
I want to stop, to bask in this new glimpse of you,
a gleam that narrows as you creak the louvres shut.

Adam Piette

Wardsend

SLATE	• BLACK	• GRAVE	• STONE
DEATH	• STING	• DREAD	• MOULD
TIME'S	• SHORE	• LIGHT	• STILL
SLEEP	• SLOPE	• MIND'S	• DARKS
GHOST	• SCARP	• STONE	• VOICE
OTHER	• SHINE	• BLACK	• SKIES
ENDED	• SOUND	• FREAK	• HEART
NIGHT	• BEATS	• MANIC	• STONE
BLIND	• EARTH	• WORMY	• WILDS
BLACK	• CLOUD	• BLACK	• BLOCK
FIRED	• HANDS	• KNIFE	• FALLS
MINDS	• BLANK	• GRASS	• MOUND
MOON'S	• SCARS	• STEEL	• DREAM
HELL'S	• MOUTH	• SMOKY	• HILLS
DUSTY	• DREGS	• STONE	• BLACK
METAL	• WATER	• RIVER	• BRICK
MARSH	• LUNGS	• SOOTY	• HEART
SIGHT	• FILMS	• SOUND	• STILL
GRAVE	• SCREE	• STONE	• WORLD
BLACK	• TIMES	• STONE	• WARDS

Gravesend

West End Nights

North-South moving East

UPPER HANGOVER STREET

DON'T FEEL WELL STREET

EUPHORIA STREET

CRAVE A DISH STREET

REEK AND FERMENT STREET

WELL SPENT STREET

FITZ-HIC! STREET

SLOE GIN STREET

NEWCASTLE BROWN STREET

BLOODTEST FAILED STREET

WRECKED SINGSONG STREET

ROCKING HOME STREET

O MUVVER STREET

FALLOVER LANE

S I C K F I E L D S

West-East moving South

BLADDERED	LANE		

ALL-LUVVERLY-GROOVY	ROAD	

PORT	AND	BABBLE	STREET

TRIPPING	LANE

THE	PITS	STREET

HOBBLING	STREET

GOD	WHAT	SLOP	ROAD

WASTED	STREET

CAN'T	QUITE	WALK

HEAVEN'S	SHAME	STREET

DOUBLE	VISION	STREET

John Quicke

Above Beauchief Abbey

To find this, here, above the Abbey
– a buried box, antenna rusty but intact,
behind a nettle screen, locked in by hawthorn,

its concrete outcrops painted one coat white,
the vents and entrance blocked – is to stumble
upon an old fear, to shiver at the thought

– a 'warning sequence', identification
and assessment, the blast, height and angle
of the flash, the zone, the measurement of fallout;

then to emerge after the all clear, to stare
across the flaming meadow, across the last
joke of the ha ha, the fallen Hall and its estate,

the spread of lethal snow on fairways, towards
the Abbey finally dissolved. And though
this fear has passed is there still sense enough

to heed what might be other warning signs
– self-scourging in the chapter-house, yellow
fever death reminder on a gravestone,

Hall logo for electronic data processing,
chemical treatments on fine cut grass near
wind-smacked conifers, and to the north,

hoots for the tunnel, preparation for dark moments,
last sight of the light on the river, the absence
of echo amongst thin oaks in steep woods?

Karl Riordan

Stars

I am sat at the table with Kieran,
helping him make a spyglass
out of cardboard toilet roll holders.
I keep the scissors out of his reach
but let him hold two tubes in place
while I wind tape around clockwise.
We've got enough to see into the future.

Will he focus on the way he'll fold his suit,
lining up the creases of his trousers
before having to feel his way around her,
listening to tomorrow's bus fare drop
onto the floor of a darkened lodging room?

Or the way he'll walk past his door
counting up loose change, whistling
past two braying heavies and a suit,
have to push himself through the back privet
getting his *best fucking jacket* snagged?

The pans he'll have to scrub 'til breathless,
stealing one piece of cutlery each day,
slipping a point of Sheffield Steel up t'cuff
or the time he'll explode at the funeral
for the priest referring to his mother as Dot.

Talking of dots, we couldn't skip over
the art room and the way Indian ink
will blemish his knuckles like dice pips,
tugging cuffs years later at interview
pinned to the wall by a panel of *twats*.

He'll get a laugh in the assembly hall though,
as his hand slips through the neck hole
of an emu glove-puppet, poking through the curtain
behind the headmaster and police officer,
addressing cross-legged children
drawing snakes and spots on their mate's back.

Maybe he'll find his girl held by another,
at nearly thirty he might climb up trees
shouting out at her, never to be heard.
I know that echo can last for years.
I offer glue and silver glitter
but Kieran whacks his telescope in two.

Out of Water

Not expecting to find two common ducks
coupied down behind shrubs
adjacent to Sheffield City Hall –
an old snap-box of water beside her.
The drake's shutter eyes blink sperm white to dark –
sleeping seconds to being on watch.

I'm jittery through lack of Jesus' blood,
three benches along, a near drunk couple
take their seats, a bottle of *Frosty Jack's*
passed hand to hand between them
sucking the blue out of plastic in ticks.

Duck ruffles her collar to back feathers,
head rotates and snuffs the clapper-board bill
into down as a breeze makes us all shiver.

Maurice Riordan

Badb

I was walking where the woods begin
with an almost sheer drop to the river
– so that I was eye level with the tops
of nearby trees and higher than the branch
when I came upon the crow sitting there,
so close I could have touched her with a stick.
She was creaturely and unwary, as the wind
bore her away and brought her back.
We shared the same tangy woodland smells,
the same malt-pale October sunlight.
Then I must have made a sound,
for she came alert and looked at me.
And, in that interval before the legs
could lift her weight from the branch,
as the beak sprang open to deliver
the single rough vowel, she held me off
with a look, with a sudden realignment
of the eyes above the gorping mouth.
It is the look known to legend and folk belief
– though also an attribute useful for a bird
without talons or guile to defend it.
Then she was gone, in a few wing beats
indistinguishable from her fellows wheeling
above the trees, carrying on their business,
neighbourly and otherworldly.

Peter Riley

from *On the Hermit's Cave at Cratcliffe Tor*

Crucifix and lamp niche carved in the wall
quiet breathing slowly devolving thought
wine corks and olive pips in the ash heap
soft singing, dry powder, global home.

Prevent me from disheartening, spread
my thought into result seal my song
in a small pot my heel turning on the ground
at the centre, where the sky sits.

Night closes in, heat lifts from the valley floor
the stars reappear, the grasses part
and they enter the earth, the sung men.
The traders, burdened with a constant elsewhere.

Crucifix and oil stoup
in the gritstone wall
a floating wick, turning
shadows. The book
sings itself into the sack of grain
the owl at the door
and the washing-up to be done.

Gladly, willingly, free of guilt
free of not-guilt, fixing
sequences across
distant points, where
shadows gather, where
the living trade, and sing
their lives into the earth.
Everything I do is that song's descant.

The broken pot in the grave
outside the front door
what you might wish to become:
shadows on the sea,
a stronghold sure.

Cross and cup scooped
in the living stone
in the earth, elsewhere.

For equity, for spread of gain
raise the white stone, the red
light on the shore where
the merchant ship rounds the headland.

Two pale lines on the ground
over the hill's shoulder
the returning workman catches
the song in the night
from the wooded hillside
a faint light among the trees,
owl and badger signalling
beyond their species.

Intimately, in the village, turn
the dance, the baby's head towards.

Rony Robinson

Evensong, S 17

Years later
We meet at the theatre
Me and the vicar's high school daughter
She pretends we didn't know each other

It was the twenty-fifth Sunday after Trinity
So a little early for all my Christmases to come at once
And for such an epiphany,
The evensong the vicar's high school daughter broke my voice.

6 Laverdene Drive Totley Sheffield Yorkshire England Europe
Northern Hemisphere The World The Milky Way The Universe

2
4
Us

8
10
12
14

      7
      5
      3
      1.

Bailey
Judge
Us

Brown
Marsh
Turton
Paskin

    Hogg
    Bottom
    Waterfall
    Not sure.

Little mester and wife
Wages clerk and wife
Us

Gardener and wife
Engineer and wife
Salesman, wife, son
Policeman, wife, son

    Lazy man, wife, four kids
    Mother, daughter
    Shop assistant, wife, son, daughter
    Two old people.

A couple who can't have a baby because
Her sister next door has her thyroid
Us

A wife who only talks when he isn't in
A couple who take turns in their deckchair
A couple who call their hut Chatsworth and keep beer in it
A husband who looks in bedrooms

    An adopted husband who plays on his own with the toys
    A mother and daughter who aren't allowed men
    A wife and daughter who get cross
    Two old people.

Mrs Bailey loved little Mester Bailey and laughed at his little joke
Mrs Judge couldn't be a real wife to Mr Judge because of her thyroid
Us

Mrs Brown squeaked in their lavatory
Mrs Marsh lost their child and didn't know where to find it
Mrs Turton's Roger had webbed fingers
Mrs Paskin got mistaken for the Queen Mother

     Mrs Hogg tried her best
     The Misses Bottoms drove off with the Conservatives
     Mrs Waterfall wanted her own path
     Two old people.

He died
He died
Us

She died
He died
He died
He died

     She died
     She died
     He died
     They probably died.

what the important men of sheffield do every first monday
of every month

my dad goes into a room
and some important men kneel him down
to make him indigent
then he has to rip his shirt open
so they can prickle his nipple with a sword

then he has to put on an apron to catch the blood
and then he is blindfolded
so they can tickle a dagger on his neck
then wrap him in a shroud
and pretend he's dead
only you can get your charlie chopped off
and buried a cable's length from the sea at bridlington at low tide
if you tell anyone

and he told me

and he told me the names of all the other important men who do it still
and some of them are
captain scott of the antarctic and
captain webb off of the matchbox
gene autry, mozart, don bradman
houdini, gilbert of gilbert and sullivan
my headmaster and christopher wren
and hardy of laurel and
and
buffalo bill
and now I've told you
so you can get your charlie chopped off too

Shelley Roche-Jacques

Civic Space
after Katherine Mansfield

The Casual Play Worker calls them round:
These are plants the dinosaurs ate.
We are going to paint them – wait!

But they're bursting full of squawks
and drop haphazardly in groups
across the sunny glasshouse paths.

Above, in the arid, open space
great blades cut time, cool and precise.
Cameras on arched beams swivel and shine.

Next door they're building a hotel.
A yellow crane robustly hoists,
egg-yolk hardhats scoot below.

Back down here on the hothouse floor
Soup of the Day is Organic Carrot.
Lunch-breakers absentmindedly navigate.

A City Centre Ambassador
stands blinking by the refreshment bar,
her City Council insignia

flaring now and then in the filtered sun.
She waits, packed up with civic knowledge.
The place will shut at 5 o'clock.

Meanwhile the pre-school pterodactyls
squabble and swoop over yellows and greens.
One of them squeals through the cycad leaves

seeing the glaring gold eye of a *big* dinosaur!
Another stares upwards silently watching
the crane swing its load like the meteor.

Building

Crossing the ocean sealed in a tin can is no fun:
the darkness and nausea – dread of it coming to an end.
Everything piecework of the shuddering torchlight,
blind trust in the bastards to remember something
is breathing down in the hold. Thank Christ today
I work the skyline, bolstered by the noisy air.

When the lorry doors were levered open
we arched and scrambled like cats from a sack.
But from up here, looking back; better that
we were uncovered – questioned for hours
about home and why we left and why we came.
For the first time someone writing it down.

I said to myself come Hell I was not going back.
I would find a thing to do. Never frightened by heights,
as a child from the top of the tallest tree
I gazed down on the mischief of others:
the sleights of women, lies of men,
the pedlars' bells and curses rising up to me.

The date of my hearing slipped – kept sliding
until one day someone with a suit and committee
signed a treaty ... that changed things for me.
Rules were translated to the language of my country.
Since then I must have rendered half this city
and the drills ring in my head now like a charm.

With Roses and Locomotives

You hear the Rosa Banksiana's perfect miniatures
are blooming now in gardens further south,
and even here in the long-row shadow of our terrraced street
backyards are again made durable, re-hung with Spring and dusk.
But hold still a while, breathe, and do not make a scene.

The spiders may be arch high-wire and spin;
lavish acrobats, thinking nothing of autumn,
vibrissal twitching behind the seedlings mean
we're fixed a moment, weighed, then left to be,
but not everything is such bewitched succession.

Look up to the backs of these houses either side.
You know the slow stew of privacy,
staid shapes obscured by bathroom glass.
Further off an attic window's tilt
lets out the mute electric of a train set.

You cannot be El Greco, a hot-dog eating contest,
or ticker tape parade. These things are larger than you
and met with suddener – will always cause more fuss
among a certain type of scarf-wearer – Niagara Falls
to the whinnying of the old stone water feature.
Do not complain to your neighbours, nor of them,
nor put on the hat of the plumed white elephant.

Instead return to that attic window, slip us through
to the painstaked intimacy of the model railway:
a countryside, a puddle-town of shops with awning,
a market day and level crossing, where a figure,
brusque as a rose and eyes picked out in sterling grey,
stands, blunted hands thrown up, at the locomotive's dash
for the null of the tunnel he cannot stop.

Ann Sansom

Crooks

in Crookes of all places; as far removed as you could move
from this red-light dive, dealers jostling punters outside
Caesar's Sauna, go tooled up to the chip shop
nobody in their right mind postcode. We like it.

But then this street's the curve on the figures,
hemmed in as it is by St Jude's and the vicarage.
You're asking for it, if you ask me, cosying into a district
noted for its rectitude, its niceness.

I've found it's often safer in the thick of thieves,
sharing the guttering with robbers. Good fences
make good neighbours, especially if
they're your uncles, brothers, nephews. Family,

I'm all for it; Love and Hate tattooed on knuckles.
You know where you stand on Paradise Road, Belle Vue.
Remember the estate named after poets:
Wordsworth for the problem families, De Quincey

for smack-heads. Place names are more of a request
than a label, a sign of what's lacking. Look at Hawes.
So to move up to Crookes, and then go all astounded
when you turn the key on nothing left, everything

binbagged and changing hands
before you've hardly caught the bus ...
I'd come home if I were you.
It's where the heart is.

Peter Sansom

July Football at Abbeydale Park

What was me and Tom playing three-and-in's
become twenty-odd of us, toddlers to grown men
up and down the twilight in slip-on (off) shoes
or Beckham 7 shirts and Nike boots, oblivious
to the swifts and/or bats and the brilliant armada
of hot air balloons over Attercliffe.
The swings at the far end are deserted now
of teenagers with their cans; a dog-walker
shouts at a bush; and at once the crown green's
empty, most of them in the Tollgate
where Roy will be thinking of calling time.
At the offy too Shaheena's slotting the grilles
onto the windows, though she'll stay open
till they turn out, which means we can stop
on our way back, clarted up and dripping with sweat,
for milk and bread and nearly yesterday's paper.

Seni Seneviratne

Spem In Alium – Motet For 40 Voices
(Millenium Gallery – Sheffield)

The boy's ear is close to a speaker, he laughs,
skips away, then back, away, then back, away
like a firefly, his red jacket illuminating the room

His girlfriend's rose-coloured dreads are gathered
in bunches and she runs at him, jumps, hugs him
in the centre of this circle of speakers.

The music stops. I wait. I listen to the cough
and shuffle of voices waiting to begin again.
The excited couple run from speaker to speaker.

I watch the effect of sound on them as I feel its
effect on me. They are moving sculptures in this
installation of sound, treading diverse harmonies,

while the curator sleeps in the corner.

Susan Shaw

Five Sheffield Snapshots

Wishes pile and spill,
burdening cubed fountains with
coins thrown, flipped and spun.

Town hall clock strikes twelve,
city pauses; peregrine
owns the steel-domed sky.

Chatelaine chain swings
hip-high miniatures to snip,
lock, seal, slice and stitch.

Names wear smooth with soles
of shoppers' shoes; cathedralled
hush empty within.

Spoons' shapes shift slowly,
embossed, pierced, engraved, impressed;
they outlive us all.

Watersmeet

Queen of the wasteland,
Buddleia shoots honeyed blooms
beyond the culvert's arch.
Two rivers converge cautiously below,
peat-brown Don diffusing,
transparent Sheaf diluting.

One flow emerges seamlessly,
grown shallow under Blonk Bridge.
Like a bride, Sheaf surrenders her name,

speeded, guided and channelled by Don
with a promise of safe passage:
to Dutch River, to Humber, to the sea.

Aerial

Vulcan takes aim,
pits his wit against pigeons
splattering the parapets.
Peregrine searches, splits the skyline;
arrows back wings to knock a dove down.

Workers feed from sandwich boxes
while shoppers search sale windows.
Peregrine strips flesh in the statue's shadow,
releasing spiralled feathers from the roof tops;
a small girl considers the empty sky.

Diana Syder

from *The Edges:*
Burbage Rocks, Ringinglow

moon

Its slow traverse
of the cliff face
has entered the rock
as a slight unsettling
of electrons
to the right or left,
a rhythm of quartz.

The moon is a dull lamp
in deep stone
tugging at the dead weight
of bedrock

or a pulse
through water-filled seams
with molecules dragged
one way and then the other
by a harsh moon sea
casting its shadows

or an afternoon moon
chased silver blue against
the chalky flats of the sky.

The moon prints itself.
The moon prints itself

is how moon is remembered.

rain

Rock shines.
Water is a way to listen.
Echo spatters on echo
and slams in clouds
down the valley.

The driven rain dissolves
elephantine greys,
waterlogged clays,
an entire serene
and plodding chemistry
of endurances
in which crystals
are translated
into sinuous currents.

Deltas of water
flood and drain.

Run off and spate,
how rain is remembered.

wind

Clamour and fracture,
a major to minor shift
in the shriek of gullies
and cloughs, barbed wire
and broken fences.

With the storm at full height,
all the muscles
of the valley grab at it,
slab upon slab
of noise tumbles down
from the turbulence
of open country

then dropping
out of the wind,
the cliff's sudden silences.

Rib bones rock on the turf,
a section of spine strung
between reed clump and heather.
Scraps of fleece and sheep shit
catch in the cracks
where grit scours nooks
and crannies deeper.

By the grind of sediment
is wind remembered.

cliff

I am outcrop, edge, crack,
ledge, overhang, gully,
sheer face, slab and cleft,
I am rubble and scree,
wet grit, gravels
and course blown sand.
This occupies me.

The filmy universe flies past
or undone by the evening sun
I melt in the distance.

Moon is a ghost,
midnight a blue chill
scratched onto silicates.
Morning is a sheer drop.

The massive epochs
are gathered behind.

I lean into the day.

David Tait

Self-Portrait with God

Walking downtown in the small hours
in the fog, kicked out before the first train

when the only thing to do is walk
these quiet roads, the last tram clanking

towards its depot, the buses abandoned
at their terminals, my head fat with drink

veering from pavement to pavement
across emptied streets towards the river

lying hushed in the mist, the only light
emitting from skyscrapers, the town hall,

a casino that seems down on its luck.
I have always lived by water

in houses where windows open wide enough
to carry a spray of their patter,

so when I choose a new place to live
a walk by a beck or bridge over a stream

is often foremost in my head. The river tonight
though seems as restless as a ghost on a chair,

as though it too dreams of the clatter
of rain, of passage from one place to the next,

of being lifted with violence
and flung out towards the city. Here's a story:

a friend of mine, a guide in the lakes
takes tourists up a famous fell.

On windy days the ridge is impassable
and on this day the group crouched

as one at the foot of the hill and watched gales
lift up and hurl water from the tarn

at the mountain. He told me it looked
like baptism performed by a whirlwind

though nobody's camera could capture the shot.
For me, it is moments like that, moments like this

with nothing to prove or atone for, that we're closest
to whatever God we've made of our doubts,

whether kicked out into the small hours
or clambering towards the mercy of a fell.

And in either case, what can we offer but love –
love and wonder – that lift from our bodies as vapour.

Bryn James Tales

Town Planning

This man gurns
as though he is shy inside a cartoon, disabled

into its primary colour pathologies.
He gurns

        because he is missing his jaw
and the crayon aging around two gapings

onto the bench behind him
are tipping tourists towards the belly pulses

of red being alive.
I hear he is from a

catastrophe cemetery; neat rows of bodies
        at clock angles like fish scales

against a deck palette
        the fanning of portobello, division streets

the careful fanning of the fingers which
place his body into wearing its rust

into the hunch of his disapproval
at the state of our sterile world:

very sobering, very sobering,
we don't like an inch of snow.

        In front of the awful fuming nothing
underneath his teeth, we retreat into romances

devise pollens of gold to prick his miasma,
smashed stamens for the ghost fact of his corpse

bitten shovels that rushed and slumped
when the city kept going

towards us

Can He Roll Back the Ocean to its Springs?

government broke up in the past few minutes

E'en thus she charm'd the country
with a weeping sister.
                            Home wept,

treated in hospital, just as if they
policemen had been
after midnight, then spun slim films.

We will be here as long as
a police officer's ten thousand years ago;

and his camera
                            around th' Almighty's form,
changed and cold;

build this new facility He said,
A pensive hue. Equipment destroyed. Still

No project cannot happen,
                            your loved flowers assume.

Than All Earth's Monsters Heretofore Have Made

O bid him welcome then!
mechanical engineer.
around thee, for a world most palpable

Oh, anger is of shapeless ghosts,
being heckled and even;
resident

and let his eyes at riot,
roof'd by the cloud which cast his frown
lead to a town

of firebombs and rocks o'er Midhope,
gloom o'er Tankersley, with red
masked youths hurled

Sarah Thomasin

Be Frit, Be Reight Frit

The waters they are rising from five rivers
A mighty beast dwells deep within the Don
For fifty thousand years he's slumbered on
But now his scaly body twists and quivers

A child looks into the depths and shivers
It seems as though the sun has never shone
On waters that are rising from five rivers
A mighty beast dwells deep within the Don

The rain comes down in savage silver slivers
Soon everything in Sheffield will be gone.
Each café, supermarket and salon.
Oblivion is what the beast delivers
The waters they are rising from five rivers.

Mothertongue

Born an outsider, I suckled familiar vowels
From my mother, who nourished her Yorkshire born child with the sounds
She was raised on, swaddled me close from the brisk, sharp speech
Of our neighbours, created a tiny reminder of home
Lisping and babbling the way the babies did back in the town
Where she grew up.

Born in this county, but never quite seeming to fit
With the others, who laughed at the lass who talks funny.
With a language which struggled and fought with my fragile tones
And too slowly to hear as it happened, the change had begun.
As my accent got broader I slowly moved further away from a town
Where I never grew up.

Katharine Towers

Farm Diary

Upper Booth, January 9th 1877

Levi says we have two sheep dead
at Edale Head, one more in the long field.

He says the frost has nailed their fleeces to the grass,
so they'll have to stay where God put them.

I can't remember any harder winter,
my hands old from breaking frozen water

and when I wake my breath in webs across my mouth.
We took a cart for wood to Gorsey Side –

our horses looked as proud as Roman soldiers
in their harnesses. Levi wants to trim

the fallen trees for making spokes and edgestakes
and for an everlasting fire. The Bible says

*weeping may endure for a night but joy cometh
in the morning*, and so do I believe.

John Turner

Sheffield Village

Sheffield is not a city
In which to bury your sins.
Random encounters
Occur daily
In every supermarket
Across town.
Vague acquaintances are able to provide
A detailed catalogue of your movements
Over the last 4 years.
You meet a former neighbour
Who has recently married your work colleague.
Your daughter's friend is there with her mother
Who, it turns out, was your lover, briefly, in the 1980s.
Your best friend in the 1970s
(Who played ukelele in your folk band)
Has retrained, it seems –
And now manages the store ...
You fix a tight smile
And exaggerate your current life successes.
Your old friend nods quietly.
He looks over his shoulder
Curiously
At you
As you leave the store.

On The Edge

The houses lie
Behind trees
And wide hedges
In leafy streetscapes.
In Nether Edge
The people sit happily
By their windows
Behind lace curtains,
Sharing stories of the day.
The neighbourhood group
Drink green tea together
In Café No. 9 –
Across the road from the Bowls Green.

Every once in a while,
There is a noise from the streets –
Residents draw back the curtains
And peer outside.

Today, it is The Farmer's Market –
Nether Edge is alive, the streets sing,
The pavements throb ...

Go to Nether Edge –
Take the 22 bus
And arrive at the crossroads ...

Hunters Bards

The streets are a stage
In Hunters Bar.
Cyclists in their helmets
And luminous jackets
Speed past you,
Overtaking the runners
In full athlete's gear.
Guitar-players
Are lodged in shop doorways
And young men act out
Loud conversations
Near the bus stop.
There is no need to sleep
In Hunters Bar,
Life is 24/7...
And the entertainment is free.

Carolyn Waudby

Wardsend*

The lads bear me –
hefters of hammers,
muck under the nails.

Women washed me
but soap and scrub could not shift it –
I wear it with my Sunday suit.

We cross. The river
has no sound, runs hot.

I am ready – know
the deafening din of the dark,
the white melt.

* The name Wardsend is believed to be derived from World's End.

Song of the Nepr*

breast hot see
my hair
darkness

mist
rapids
grass
        springing

summon the wind
cross
scream
my breast hot

storm
shadow
teeth

tread
fear
drool

your fingers
in my hair

*nepr – a pagan word meaning 'water spirit' and possible origin of the name Neepsend.

River Don

Today, I hope to remain undiscovered –
Peace. Almost silence. The stillness
of stopping.
It is I who drives the wheel.
The world comes to me –
sun, clouds, trees,

paper, curses, whispers.
I do not let them in,
send them back.

Christine Webb

A Sheffield Man

Every morning my grandfather, lying in bed
or for all I know kneeling beside it,
would pray to become a better man,
then button up his shirt, lace his boots, set out
breathing the sharp reek of the morning –
rain on the field-path, sea-spray, the city's steel fume –
to become a better labourer, soldier, tram conductor.
Daily he resumed the wrestle with God in his head,
hammered the hot metal of his temper and ambition,
asking Can I be a better union man today,
better husband, father? In a fury of love
he carved from the joint the choicest slice,
always, for his wife, and once in winter
when she demurred at the cost of new slippers
he seized the old ones and flung them on the fireback.
Each Sunday he cooked a pan of sausages and gravy
before cleaning seven pairs of shoes for chapel
where he sang his favourite hymn and dared
any of his daughters to laugh at Jesus' bosom.
Returning, he saw the city's barefoot children,
the thin faces, the legs bent with rickets,
urging him to be a better councillor, negotiator –
more eloquent, more ingenious. Begin again,
his heart told him. Begin again.

Linda Lee Welch

my feet won't let me

I'm walking the rim
of the steep-sided bowl that holds
the dam
                        teetering
between the dry hills and the drowning

something's down there in the water calling
but when I feel like falling in

Dam Flask

The first real chill
of autumn means
I head out, heart
pumping with change
the muscularity of it
the signalling thrill,

into this wood
these trees
so staunch and settled
turning golden
with their hands up
to the sky

A sapling
in their sheltering
arms, I'll never
get that tall
or live
that long.

Rivelin June

Electric pulsing green shoots from the trees
It hits my heart with dazzling aplomb
I stumble in the tingling of the breeze
I can't imagine where the winter's gone

It hits my heart with dazzling aplomb
It fills the fizzing morning with delight
I can't imagine where the winter's gone
I'd gotten used to living without light

It fills the fizzing morning with delight
I'm dizzy with the colour of the day
I'd gotten used to living without light
This buzzing brightness takes my breath away

I'm dizzy with the colour of the day
The rushing of the river in my ears
This buzzing brightness takes my breath away
The crunching weight of winter disappears

The rushing of the river in my ears
I stumble in the tingling of the breeze
The crunching weight of winter disappears
Electric pulsing green shoots from the trees

At the Weir

I left some silver by the weir
(It's not so often I come here, but did
today)
I leaned, and couldn't see my face
but I saw yours (I didn't know
you'd come along)
I felt your fingers brush my flesh

my pearly lobe all trembling
Everyone I know's in Perth
or Thailand, jumping out of planes
or deep-sea diving
I'm beside the River Don at Walk Mill Weir
with vertigo, and naked ear, searching –
but (your voice still here)
words like splash, split, splay
intrude, and I can't get away

Ben Wilkinson

Perspective

*commissioned for Poems On The Trams as part of imove, Yorkshire's cultural
programme for London 2012*

What makes a city is what you make of it.
Its heartbeat's like a bassline, true and quick.
Watch how it pulses with the lives we live –
living side-by-side, each of us different.
Now for the odd fight or clash or cruel word
that spills onto streets, there's someone helping
another, just trying to make ends meet.
Sneer, if doubt says you won't buy into this,
but know these words aren't selling anything.
Find a window seat on the tram or bus.
See the sun splinter through the clouds above.
See the bustle, the people, the endless roads,
the details. Step off at a different stop.
See the city again from that distant hilltop.

Sunday

The rain lashing down like a TV's static
as smokers huddle under pubs' lintels –
from the Lescar across to Porter Cottage
the storm turns from drizzle to dismal.
Bless he who, with the cool persistence
of a craftsman, re-rolls a soggy Rizla;
opening the botched attempt in silence
as he rolls it into another.

When I leave with Jes, the sky has cleared:
a van trundles down Sharrowvale past
the shell of a butcher's, boarded and barred;

the sun and bulky nimbus in weird contrast
as I open up the Marlboros, offer her one,
struggling to recall if it was accident or arson.

The River Don

                        rushes by, a sudden current pushing on
past rows of fig trees blooming from its banks
and factories' warm outfalls, spilling nearby.
Remember how the floods two years back
rose to the mark etched on The Fat Cat's wall;
that third summer of ours when the rain did
nothing but pour, and the thought of what we
might wake to was the dream I'd been suffering
on/off for weeks?
                        It never reached us. We didn't
climb downstairs, half-asleep, to find our furniture
floating or ornaments, CDs and old cassette tapes
making their bids to escape. Instead, the house
sat safe and sound – floors dry, photo frames still,
something else edging closer, the way that water will.

Noel Williams

Allotments

These ramshackle scraps of straggled gardens:
his Sherwood, Eldorado, Hy-Brasil.
Under the autumn smoke of coke and burning leaves
he tracked and compassed, sword in hand.

He'd break through hedgerow, battle bindweed
shred lupins' caterpillar pods of raindrops,
creep up on old man crab,
unweigh his knotty fruit of breeding wasps.

The burr of a bee teasing petticoats of buddleia
might be a bomb the blitz forgot.
Or he might wrench a tin ad for Henderson's
from its thorn doorway and slither down the bank.

He never saw fat leaves of rhubarb slug-rid,
heard no alarm of hidden wings.
These strangled paths of spindly thistles
mapped his town on a sunlit page.

Ox Stones

A thumb traces the skin of the shoulder
of the first stone, its scapula
burning as ice burns,
as if there are stars pricked in gritstone,
their furnace collapsed into crystal chill.

So they crouch, dumb bulls, unsensing,
as the wind flirts or sneers,
as the frost works its sly wedges,
as the rain wheels in swarms of scribing drops;

stare across the moor, blind
to a child mired thigh deep,
scowl, deaf to the howl of parents,
where heather shouts its scent around them.

If smoke or dawn warms the city,
if heat lifts ghosts from the tarmac,
if a passing step flushes song from a skylark,
they'll herd storms in from the hill.

Overlooking Baker's Hill

I see them where they never stood
above these tessellated steps,
a staircase steeply doubled back
cupping the tread of decades.
Hand in hand: brother – father – brother.
His heavy yellow fists rough comfort
for their mittened fingers.
Through railings ungreened by rust they gaze
exactly as they never did, the folded stair dropping
into a tide of mailvans and sidings.

They'd not hear him talk of the systole
and diastole of stoker and bellows,
the town's long shovel of coke into the crux of fire,
the drawl of liquid iron from furnace
with a flare to scald eyes or sear a beard bald
as they watched the shoving engines drip steam
like lace across the marshalling yards.

Down by The Penny Black and Pond Hill,
he'd load dreams on each flatbed and truck.
Nothing he might say touched the secret ponds
under the skin and sinews of railway tracks.
No hint of a landfilled future,
the sump of slag and pig-iron dumped
in artery and lung.

Tony Williams

The Looking Behind Walls Club

The Looking Behind Walls Club
lost its headquarters today: it got too familiar to the members
and dissipated into their sad knowledge of the city.
It didn't make the papers. It wasn't their sort of story:

all footnote, no beginning, no middle, no end. So it ended. We stood around,
trying to avoid conversation, coughing, poking, looking, till we saw someone coming,
and hid, I don't know why, inside a disused shed, then lost
an hour or two rummaging through knick-knacks and pots of two-stroke.

We look for lost traces, evidence of things, stuff, items, objects, trinkets,
crap, phenomena, dead-end versions; mistake empty crisp packets
for the Grail's wrapper. What's that hidden down there under the chipboard flooring?
Bluebeard's hoard? Chickenfeed? The Treasure of the Sierra Madre?

The left and forgotten down-at-heel site of foxgloves, broken boxes,
a flat football, two mouldy canvas shoes, who knows, a stash of street signs
from the 1930s, is our open-air cathedral. We only ever pray for distances,
unknowns, new anonymities and elsewheres as habitat. Hallelujah! No one hears us.

Sneak down the side of the old canal, snub the footpath.
Meet me under the bridge like pottering urban trolls, or
vault the chain-link into the sub-station's gravel yard for no good reason,
or anywhere. Don't tell me postcodes, addresses, la-la-la I can't hear you.

Describe it to me. Its nameless locations, where it leaves the track, the shape of its nothing,
its colours of neglected grimes, the feel of moss on your fingers.
What songbirds weren't singing there. Micro-climate, geology. How many minutes
you wasted. Whisper it, don't write them down. Someone might use it.

This club's no fun any more. Too organised. We burn the rolls. Our song drifts out
one more time across a web of dusty brickwork gennels: Don't fence me in ...
We sniff the air: corroded metal, dinners, stagnant water.
Always another wall to look behind. The unknown region slides.

Late Schoolboys

The speed of their gallows walk's
lower even than their backpacks,
slung pained and aslant like their
dissenting grimaces. Trudging, more

stop than start, they take long-cuts
in twos and threes through the drab bits
of scrub tacked on to public parks,
meet the dogs on their walks

and their stoic, indifferent owners. Some
lost glove rots in front of them
all winter, and they know each flake
of paint on the railings their sticks rattle.

They'll arrive in a ragged parade
that mourns into the school's facade
and wait for the worst to burst over them
in a spat shower of opprobrium.

The birch, the worn footpath's line,
the pavements and tarmac patches they learn
over years of yawns and missed breakfasts,
the dread of the official lists,

are not on the syllabus;
nothing that interests them is.
They know only the equation of day
and death, and they avoid it stubbornly,

rolling over on their lives
and bright futures as depressives.
They have their love affairs with sleep
and blush at Miss. They speak in burps.

Lateness is the state of grace
they travel through and in this place
where their dazed craniums
conceive the codas of their dreams

they daub their uniforms with mud
to make the powers storm and chide
and have confirmed that everyone
despises them, and they the sun.

River Wolton

Common Sense

The return leg of our last trip, moving apart,
just the hoover, one grey J-Cloth and a plant pot left,
you signal at the junction onto Burngreave Road
and straight ahead of us she staggers off the kerb,
lurches to a cab window, falls back.

I'd turn tail, leave her to the cops
but you pull over, help her to her feet.
She stinks of whisky, her whole skin's a bruise
but when you ask her where she lives,
it's the last place we'd expect.

She sits quietly on the back seat,
speaking only to apologise.
She's posh, I think, *how did she end up here?*
Then reaching for some common sense, I ask
What's happened? Have you been to the police?

She's adamant – she brought it on herself.
We're at our best, calm
as we haven't been for months.
She hugs goodbye with tender floppy arms
and totters off, enveloped by the dark.

Sheffield – St Pancras

This is my ninetieth bisection of the Midlands.
Here is the Buffet Bar, its red formica top
over which I've leaned to indicate my choice of Kit Kat,
plastic-coated Dundee slice, free-range egg and cress
or Typhoo, which has by turns been complimentary
or one pound fifty-three. Six swans are gliding

on the burst skin of the Derwent, Liam who's four
is launching paratroop attacks throughout the Quiet Zone.

There's only ever been one train, my train.
This is the same engine that sent me north
and pulls me back for sickness, love
and obligation. This is the on-board payphone
where I called Helen to say my Dad had died
and that I'd leapt into a taxi, hurtled through the station.

This is the seat I curled up in, facing the direction
of travel, this is the stowaway grey table
with its one receding eye where I have lodged my tea
and where I write now, next to my reflection.

Witness

6.45 a.m. A parked white Transit
is not Immigration. Abdul answers the door.
Everyone's asleep. I tuck myself into the couch,
wonder how we'll stall the dawn.

In Nazaneen and Sahar's Christmas cards
Byron Wood Primary has said farewell.
Sataish's new toy-kitchen back in the box,
no food bought since last week.

We wait. Should get a removal date,
flight-time but no-one's sure.
The MP says Go quietly. Nothing
since last week when they came at 8.

The First Line buses ricochet
down Burngreave Road. Microwave pings open.
Shukriya brings spiced tea and almonds.
Sheffield. This year, this week. So far, so good.

Lightning Source UK Ltd.
Milton Keynes UK
UKOW051222270912

199618UK00003BE/4/P